A JOHN CATT PUBLICATION

ROY BLAT

SUCC

IS A JOURNEY

'This is a book of exceptional depth, breadth
and clarity – packed with inspiring examples.'

Geoff Barton
General Secretary, Association of School and College Leaders

First Published 2018

by John Catt Educational Ltd,
12 Deben Mill Business Centre, Old Maltings
Approach,
Melton, Woodbridge IP12 1BL

Tel: +44 (0) 1394 389850 Fax: +44 (0) 1394 386893
Email: enquiries@johncatt.com
Website: www.johncatt.com

ISBN: 978 1 911382 61 4

Set and designed by John Catt Educational Limited

What readers say about
Success is a Journey

"I always enjoy Roy Blatchford's common sense approach to leading schools. This collection of essays provides an invaluable insight into the most important things leaders should be doing.

So much in this book resonated with me as a leader of several schools, in particular that an education system is only as good as the teachers in it. As Roy suggests, let's never forget the importance of the training and support we provide to those who have chosen this wonderful profession."

Helena Mills CBE
Chief Executive, Burnt Mill Academy Trust, Harlow

"Roy Blatchford is writing at the top of his game: a voice of reason and influence in English education. Whilst we go through some very challenging times, his thoughts and words in 'Success Is A Journey' remind us why we have all committed ourselves to supporting young people so that their life chances improve."

Nick Caulfield
Principal, Ditton Park Academy, Slough

"Roy Blatchford's latest collection of essays, standards and tools is a welcome addition to the literature on educational excellence. The writing is an effervescent fizz of fresh ideas, creative thoughts and provocative proposals. Every school leader and anyone interested in how we create a climate for excellence should read this."

Rachel Macfarlane
Director of Education Services, Herts for Learning

"This is a book of exceptional depth, breadth and clarity. Rooted in an authentic knowledge of leadership and pedagogy in the UK and overseas, it contains insights that sometimes provoke and sometimes reassure us.

Roy Blatchford's observations, nudges and challenges are always rooted in an optimistic faith in teachers and leaders to enrich the lives of children and young people. In 'Success is a Journey' – packed with inspiring examples – he explains how. This is a book to read and re-read."

Geoff Barton
General Secretary, Association of School and College Leaders

Think Different

'Here's to the crazy ones.

The misfits.

The rebels. The troublemakers.

The round pegs in the square holes.

The ones who see things differently.

They're not fond of rules.

And they have no respect for the status quo.

You can quote them, disagree with them,

glorify or vilify them.

About the only thing you can't do is ignore them.

Because they change things.

They push the human race forward.

While some may see them as the crazy ones,

we see genius.

Because the people who are crazy enough to think

they can change the world, are the ones who do.'

Steve Jobs, Apple 1997

CONTENTS

INTRODUCTION

Part One is a collection of essays about the UK and international education landscape which were first published in a range of media outlets.

They are reprinted here more or less in their original texts, and sharp-eyed readers will detect an occasional repetition of my favourite phrasing. Some essays date back a few years, covering themes close to my heart. Many were written over the past 24 months while I have been working overseas on education system reform.

Does distance lend enchantment, as the old saying goes?

Certainly being away from the UK scene has given an alternative and cherished perspective, and driven an underlying imperative that it is important to value what we have. Sadly, we live in an age when the default position of pundits, journalists and social media commentators seems to be one of destructive criticism.

What I see around the world in many places is political leaders' very high regard for education in the UK – and their desire to emulate its great strengths in their own countries. This applies equally to early years, primary, secondary and higher education.

There are 35 essays in *Success Is A Journey*. An essay, deriving from its French origin, is an *essai*, an 'attempt' to rehearse an idea. It weighs up perspectives and often comes down on one side of a debate. The words are orchestrated to test the quality of an argument. The best essays do so in ways which do not waste words. Master storyteller Roald Dahl says about the great short story: 'there's no time for the sun filtering through the pine trees.'

We all have stories to tell, and in the words of Irish author John Banville, 'the past beats inside us like a second heart.' In essence, writing is editing and in that spirit this collection adopts a less-is-more approach. What is gained in brevity may be lost in depth. I leave that to the reader to judge.

One further reflection: I observe in one of the essays that it is a feature of the modern era that 'the extraordinary becomes the commonplace at a faster and faster rate'. As a contemporary essayist, one runs the risk of making statements which later appear either foolish or prescient, particularly when commenting on fluid political landscapes. Either way, I trust the reader can share with me a wry smile.

****

Part Two contains the DfE Teachers' Standards, Master Teacher Standard and National Standards of Excellence for Headteachers. Why?

The distinguished HMI Ronald Arnold taught me the phrase 'the power of the first draft'. Working in the early 1970s as Secretary to Lord Bullock's committee on 'A language for life' (Department of Education and Science, 1975), Ronald almost single-handedly drafted vast chunks of the 600-page document. He maintained that his drafting was so good that committee members feared to amend the text. The late Michael Marland, a headteacher member of the committee, told me affectionately that it wasn't quite like that, but that the first draft of the Bullock Report was indeed beautifully crafted.

My own chance to produce powerful first drafts came when serving as Deputy Chair to the Department for Education's Teachers' Standards Review in 2011, and the Headteachers' Standards Review in 2014. I am confident in saying that my fellow committee members and DfE civil servants would acknowledge my lead drafting role. While my first drafts were perhaps not in Ronald Arnold's league, they did give us much shape, style and phrasing which survive to this day in the respective Standards.

I am proud of my writing for those Reviews, the more so now because I have had the opportunity to harness their content in drafting similar Standards for teachers and principals in other countries.

It is also worth noting that an increasing number of schools and academy groups across England are using the Master Teacher descriptors as part of appraisal for their best teachers, even though they were not formally adopted by Ministers and the DfE.

For the reasons outlined above, and to offer context to essays 6 and 10, the Crown Copyright material is included here.

****

Part Three explains and exemplifies the practice of *Blinks*.

Blinks are a distinctive approach to reviewing and reporting on education settings which I have, with colleagues, established over the past 15 years in the UK and internationally.

I have written widely on the subject of school and college inspection, home and abroad, holding to the view that, in the end, restless and robust *self-evaluation* should make most external *inspection* redundant.

My conversations with students, teachers and leaders while conducting hundreds of *Blinks* have informed the content of many of the essays in this collection.

Roy Blatchford

PART ONE

LEADERSHIP

'We know so much today about the cocktail of highly effective schools: the virtuous combination of well qualified, skilled teachers motivated by clear, fair-minded and knowledgeable leadership – and everyone focused on students' well-being and all-round achievements.'

'Achieving excellence in any sphere of public life is rooted in leaders *caring* more than others think is wise and *risking* more than others think is safe. Further, excellence is rooted in leaders *dreaming* more than others think is practical and *expecting* more than others think is possible.'

'A celebrated French general was once tactlessly asked, after a famous victory, if it hadn't really been won by the second-in-command. The general thought for some time before answering: "Maybe so. But one thing is certain. If the battle had been lost, I would have lost it".'

'Never name a building after anyone living or dead. With the living, you never know what they will get up to. With the dead, imagine what skeletons might be uncovered.'

'YOU'VE GOT A LOT MORE BULL**** THAN ME'

Sir Ken Morrison, founder of the supermarket chain, called a spade a spade. Following his death, stories of his bluff Yorkshire nature have been legion. At one of the retailer's annual meetings in his native Bradford he launched a verbal assault on Dalton Philips from which the then chief executive would not recover.

'When I left work and started working as a hobby, I chose to raise cattle', the veteran grocer boomed. 'I have something like 1,000 bullocks and, having listened to your presentation, Dalton, you've got a lot more bull**** than me.'

Sir Ken eschewed the world of the City and corporate governance edicts. Memorably, he once asked why have non-executive directors when he could have checkout assistants instead. And he was never happier than when pacing stores, weaving through the aisles talking to staff and shoppers, and working out what was selling well, what was not, and why.

Reading of Morrison's style and relationship with his chief executives set me thinking how I have interacted over the years with chairs of governors.

School leaders know, in sickness and in health, that *the* critical factor in running a successful school is a flourishing professional relationship with the chair of governors or trustees. A head who does not view the chair as his or her boss usually comes unstuck. The chair may well have been the person who had the final say in your appointment, so they are rooting for you to succeed.

As a young teacher in large London comprehensives during the 1970s, I was aware of two distinguished chairs of governors: Lord Mischon at Stockwell Manor and Sir Ashley Bramall at Pimlico School. To me they were distant figures with splendid white hair, glimpsed going into the head's office for important meetings or listened to keenly on annual speech days. To everyone on the staffs they were outstanding ambassadors for comprehensive education in the Inner London Education Authority, much needed in those heady political times.

Only later in my career, interviewing the heads they worked with, did I discover just how much time and personal support Lord Mischcon and Sir Ashley gave regularly, despite their own demanding professional duties in the law and local government. These were the days of disruptive teacher union action, community tensions in the estates, stop-and-search on Brixton's streets, and IRA bomb threats to schools.

Moving in 1982 as deputy to a north London grammar-school-going-comprehensive, I encountered a set of Camden and Highgate governors not to be messed with. Their combined legal, academic and financial acumen was formidable, nay, intimidating. And then Sir Peter Newsam (retiring ILEA Chief) joined the board.

For my term as Acting Head their patience with the rookie head was invaluable. When the really sticky moment came of having to deal with the suspension of a member of staff, the chair was unfailing in helping me follow due procedures, affording timely counsel when I doubted my own abilities. Above all, I learned that the very best of governors are 'privately critical and publicly loyal' – probably *the* most important lesson for headteachers in their dealings with boards.

There were two other outstanding chairs of governors during my headship days: Robert Palmer and Chris Pym. I think it no coincidence that their peers nominated them, for both were likeable, intelligent, compassionate men. The former appointed me in Oxfordshire, the latter in Milton Keynes – both invested in me from the days we first met.

Robert Palmer was a senior officer in Thames Valley Police. Working with him for a decade was the most pleasurable professional relationship I ever enjoyed in a school. His ability to judge people whom he'd only just met and to assess the merits of any situation were remarkable. On interviews panels his dry humour used to keep everyone gently in order and constantly amused.

He taught me the Jesuit principle of leadership: it's easier to beg forgiveness than seek permission. It suited us both that he was adept at keeping his distance from the school to let me get on with things. Equally, he was always there at end of the phone: to offer advice the day a sixth former committed suicide, and on the occasion when the British National Party came leafleting students at the school gate. Of course Robert had his foibles: he was always the *Chairman*; chairs, he asserted, were for sitting on. And lighting up a favourite cigar while standing by the finishing tape on sports days used to wind up the Head of PE wonderfully!

Chris Pym appointed me to open a brand new school and learning centre – in state-of-the-art premises – which he wished to be both traditional and radical in practice and outlook. That suited 1999, on the cusp of a new century, and both our temperaments and educational intuitions. His political nous, deep knowledge of community, adroit handling of founding governors with different agendas, passion for deep learning and out-of-the-box thinking were everything the founding staff team and student body required to shape a sustainable vision.

For a few short years we chose to meet every Monday afternoon for a couple of hours in the school's café. This was a statement to staff about our partnership and provided me with a regular opportunity to sound out my latest brilliant ruse. 'Don't scare the horses', he would say, knowing how experimental we could and couldn't be with parents who wanted the best of a Buckinghamshire grammar school blended with a pioneering comprehensive.

Chris's sudden death through cancer hit me hard. At his memorial service I realised his family had lost a venerated father figure of many parts. I had lost a founding partner. The words he expressed at one of our weekly discussions stay with me. I can hear him still: 'Never name a building after anyone living or dead. With the living, you never know what they will get up to. With the dead, imagine what skeletons might be uncovered'. It is *his* imprint much more than mine that lives on in that school community today.

So I thank these chairs of governors for their distinguished voluntary service and their vital role in my own education as a head. I commend their wise words and thoughts to the current generation of school leaders. May good governance go among us.

IN SEARCH OF A LEADER

The Americans and the French have recently elected leaders, and the UK and Germany are soon to elect their own.

Elected leaders are products of their *particular* times and cultures, not leaders for all times. Elected leaders sense the mood of their people and put themselves forward with visions of better times. They tell compelling stories, paint vivid pictures of the horizon and submit to the electorates. Political leaders thrive and suffer through social media. Success or failure at the ballot box is sudden and brutal. Democracy is bloody and messy.

Principals and headteachers perform similar high-wire acts in their own rural, urban and semi-urban settings across the country. In many ways, they have manifestos with which to lead and are subject to the same pressures of success and failure. Headteachers may not face the ballot box, but the daily courts of students, parents and governors can be just as exhilarating and unforgiving.

We know so much today about the cocktail of highly effective schools: the virtuous combination of well qualified, skilled teachers motivated by clear, fair-minded and knowledgeable leadership – and everyone focused on students' well-being and all-round achievements.

That same fair-minded leadership is not afraid to challenge orthodoxies. It thrives confidently on accountability. Inspired and inspiring school leaders embrace entrepreneurial and innovative opportunities where there are evident gains for staff development and enhancing students' experiences.

Let me take four leading headteachers I have worked with and describe briefly how I see them. They share the leadership characteristics described above, yet each makes a virtue of his or her particular setting. Their names have been changed.

Julie combines a smile and inner steel that few can match. Her personal appearance is a clear message to others, and the staff's smart dress-code is evident to any visitor. Her leadership style is rooted in valuing and working through others, championing excellence where she sees it, rooting out mediocrity with equal vigour.

Experienced in rapid primary school improvement, she is a great believer in enabling teachers to observe each other, to co-teach, to come together in short, focused workshops to tweak classroom practice. Staff meetings explore best next-step marking or smart presentations on effective techniques in phonics or applied mathematics.

Julie 'catches staff at their best', with postcards in pigeon holes that note a teacher's action which has made a difference to a child. She takes photos of pupils at work, supported by a teaching assistant who is accelerating learning, and posts the photos on the school website. When she is working beyond the school she takes her teachers with her so they can share their best practice with a wider audience. She invites other heads to visit and see the school's achievements.

Andrew *is executive head of two large primary schools. He is a maverick intellectual with a passion for primary education. He relishes taking children into ways of thinking and doing which surprise them. He challenges orthodoxies.*

His schools achieve outstanding academic results alongside memorable engagement for pupils with visiting musicians, scientists, artists, playwrights and mathematicians. He makes rules to break them, creating enquiring, confident and independent learners, ready to take on the world at 11+. The inclusion work of the school is notable.

This ethos of colourful intellectual enquiry has not come about by chance. Andrew gathers around him colleagues who push boundaries with children's learning, rooted in their own fields of expertise. He visits any teachers he appoints in their current workplace; he is looking for 'can-do' people who will bring an energy, spark and perhaps a non-teaching background to the school. He spends a lot of time creating the team spirit, formally and informally.

Nicola *is an ardent advocate of single-sex education. She has a singular vision about the potency of comprehensive education in inner cities. She is a sterling critic of what she sees as an inspection regime which lets data get in the way of overall judgements about young people whose achievements against all odds are outstanding, but are not judged as such. She is as committed to the high-flyer from a favoured background as she is to searching out the potential of a looked-after child.*

18

Her annual review cycle, accompanying documentation and associated meetings with staff and governors follow a well trodden path. Each September, with a candid external eye in tow, she personally meets each head of faculty to review examination results. Each head of faculty produces an analytical report to a given format. The dialogue is warm and sharp, the head commending successes and peeling back disappointments with equal energy.

Nicola is a wise listener, takes advice from external consultants and senior colleagues, then backs her convictions. Governors trust and engage well with her strategic lead. To watch her at work balancing the headteacher's proverbial spinning plates is to appreciate the relentlessness of the role, its potential loneliness, and the resilience required for contemporary headship.

Luke enjoyed a successful career in the aviation industry prior to becoming a Future Leader and, within a short period, head of what he affectionately calls a 'bump to 16' academy: on site there is a Children's Centre, primary and secondary school, and a resource base for pupils with severe learning difficulties. He brings fresh, divergent thinking to a campus that has been steeped in educational failure, neglect and low self-esteem. Staff warm to his softly spoken manner and off-beat style of asking questions.

Rooted in his background outside the teaching profession, he has established with all staff that they need to be outward-facing, following years of inward-facing, cosy and complacent practice. His starting point has been to enable colleagues who have never visited outstanding practice to do just that, establishing a budget with governors to fund a 'visits entitlement' for staff.

Luke knows that transforming chronic under-achievement amongst pupils and challenging tired attitudes amongst staff is not a quick-fix. He has introduced day reviews of practice, led by heads of department paired up with counterparts in the same subject from a nearby secondary school. Heads of maths, science, the arts and English have reviewed each other's practices, identifying what works well and what needs to change.

Mutual challenge in a climate of mutual respect is the underpinning theme of this head's school improvement journey. He's not there yet, but he's getting there.

I wonder, of course, what these four good colleagues might be able to teach current and future political leaders.

EIGHT LEADERSHIP MAXIMS

1. Leave them with a smile on their face

Leading schools requires taking tough decisions at regular intervals. Getting the right tone with colleagues matters, especially when leaders have to convey difficult messages. There is a real knack to 'telling it like it is', and still leaving the member of staff in good spirits. Accomplished heads manage to get this right most of the time. And learn quickly when they make a mistake. 'It's not what I'm saying that matters. It's what you're hearing'.

2. Less is More

In the face of sometimes overwhelming bureaucracy, wise heads know how to cut to the chase. Emails, reports, letters of complaint, advisory notes, safeguarding updates, financial spreadsheets – the sheer volume of material can threaten to swamp. A hallmark of thoughtful leadership is the ability to sift at pace, with an eye for the important detail. Crafting one side of A4, with the right words in the right order, can be eminently more practical and accessible for any audience, whether governor, inspector or parent.

3. It's not what's in the diary that kills you, it's what is not in the diary

Headteachers' diaries can be proverbial bomb-sites. Everyone wants to see the head, right now. If you're not very careful, the urgent consumes the important. But with a full list of scheduled diary commitments, along comes something *really* urgent. The best heads have developed creative solutions to potential diary crashes, usually involving a skilled secretary, willing deputies and the occasional 'white lies'. Time juggling is part of the job: live to fight another day.

4. Leaders enable … managers control

It is a natural inclination early in a manager's career to want to control. You've been promoted so show what you can do. Observing skilled middle managers is to see them starting 'tight' then being willing to 'loosen'. And it's certainly what great heads do: appoint the right people in the right places, and let them flourish in a climate of measured risk.

All my professional life I have watched the average *manager* seek to control colleagues, while the confident *leader* is quite content for others to shine and take the plaudits.

5. Easier to beg forgiveness than seek permission

Not every leader subscribes to this so-called Jesuit principle of management. But show me a great school leader who seeks permission rather than following deep professional instinct, and I'll show you a school which risks faltering. Children get one chance, so no head compromises that basic tenet. But principled and values-led decision-making, inclusive of staff and students, creates vibrant teaching and learning communities. People don't look over their shoulders and seek permission. They occasionally have to say sorry.

6. A quick 'no' or a slow 'yes'

The old headteacher adage of 'never say yes in a corridor' probably rings true for many school leaders. Staff often want instant decisions from headteachers – and there's a place for those, for example in certain health and safety contexts. But wisdom suggests that a little time pondering with colleagues will lead to a better course of actions. Judicious timing in headship is crucial, so better a quick 'no' and slow 'yes'. The alternative can be 'command and reverse', a recipe for confusion.

7. An email is a postcard to *The Sun*

In politics, so in headship: timing and communication are everything. Contemporary headship is played out against a back-cloth of 24-hour media, Twitter and Facebook. Pupils and parents can turn a petty drama into a crisis at the flick of a thumb. Heads today spend a disproportionate amount of time picking up the pieces of poorly worded emails. Good schools and wise leaders have established clear protocols for all staff when responding to social media. *Caveat emptor* has become *sender beware.*

8. Graveyards are full of indispensable people

Spending time alongside heads in schools, helping them see afresh their daily routines, is endlessly fascinating. The best amongst them stay resolutely focused on the children they serve. Equally, they are highly skilled in identifying the next generation of leaders. Succession planning informs heads' everyday working, nudging potential future leaders to follow their instincts, to believe in their potential, to carve out ways of doing which challenge prevailing orthodoxies, to ask for forgiveness not permission.

Blink! Life goes faster than you think. Today's school leader remembers Prime Minister David Cameron's parting parliamentary words: 'I was the future once'.

DIFFERENCE BETWEEN...

A BOSS

- DRIVES EMPLOYEES
- DEPENDS ON AUTHORITY
- INSPIRES FEAR
- SAYS "I"
- PLACES BLAME FOR THE BREAKDOWN
- KNOWS HOW IT IS DONE
- USES PEOPLE
- TAKES CREDIT
- COMMANDS
- SAYS "GO"

A less productive unhappy workforce

A LEADER

- ...COACHES EMPLOYEES
- ...ON GOOD WILL
- ...GENERATES ENTHUSIASM
- ...SAYS "WE"
- ... FIXES THE BREAKDOWN
- ...SHOWS HOW IT IS DONE
- ...DEVELOPS PEOPLE
- ...GIVES CREDIT
- ...ASKS
- ...SAYS "LET'S GO"

A more productive happier workforce

DOES RECRUITMENT NEED TO BE LIKE THIS?

Saxton Bampfylde. Odgers Berndtson. Perrett Laver. Gabbitas. Heidrick & Struggles. Korn Ferry.

What do these names have in common? Legal firms from the novels of Charles Dickens? A cluster of Cotswold villages? Authors of chemistry textbooks?

They are the names of successful headhunting firms, specialising in education and the recruitment of senior leaders for leading state, independent and international schools. As you might guess, their businesses thrive. And it doesn't come cheap to secure a top principal.

Away from the headhunting arena, secondary headteacher colleagues estimate that their schools can spend in excess of £70k per annum on recruiting teachers. Primary leaders suggest the annual figure, in many areas of high teacher turn-over, is £30k plus.

The *Times Education Supplement* has enjoyed a near monopoly over many decades. One local authority recently estimated that 93% of adverts for teaching posts in its schools featured in the *TES*. National and local newspapers across the country have shared in the flow of advertising revenue. Almost none of this financial bonanza has found its way back into classrooms.

Nor have most of the profits of the many teaching agencies which now operate across the country. Typically, a school might pay an agency 25% of a first year of salary. In common with the NHS, the national education service risks being bled dry by agents' fees which divert increasingly scant resources away from the classroom.

The teaching profession has been supine for too long. Profligate spending on recruitment has to end. The school system must challenge the *status quo*, albeit belatedly. Current budget tightening should surely lead us to find different solutions. I have a few, not mutually exclusive suggestions.

1. Agents

Working with a group of deputy heads a couple of years ago discussing professional steps to headship, one entrepreneurial deputy told us that he and a colleague had set up a recruitment agency, with most of the profits channelled back into a partnership of schools. He also predicted that, over time and in common with professional football, every teacher would have an agent – and that schools would be paying those agents when teachers transferred between schools. It's heading that way. Could school partnerships and MATs establish agencies and teacher-agents whose profits are reinvested in the school system?

2. Social media

Disruptive technologies disrupt. There is a strong argument that the 'digital native' generation of teachers and school leaders can lead the way in ensuring that various forms of social media provide the 'go to' sources for online recruitment, cutting out the middle men and women. This would need co-ordinating, safeguards and due diligence. Perhaps Facebook guru and self-professing altruist Mark Zuckerberg, with his global community manifesto, might be tapped up to sponsor? Seriously, there may well be an interested social entrepreneur who could run with the idea.

3. Professional Associations

Whilst professional association and union leaders over the years have talked in my presence about cost-saving initiatives on recruitment, they have to date been sluggish on this agenda. Perhaps the entrepreneurial leadership at ASCL, combining forces with NAHT, could stake out a real intent to provide free online adverts for all primary, special and secondary leadership positions across England. Their website infrastructures already exist. And, in parallel, the merged NUT/ATL could do the same for all teaching positions. What a long overdue gift the savings would be to members wrestling with tightening budgets.

4. Department for Education (DfE)

Whilst once local authorities did much to support teacher recruitment, those days are gone. Might the DfE step in? Is it impossible to imagine a centrally funded and run online service, given every teacher in the land is registered by the Department to teach? There might indeed be added value in government being able to identify more readily where geographically, and in what subjects, teacher shortages are emerging. Or where in the country there are difficulties in securing strong middle or senior leaders. Decentralisation has been the mantra for several decades now, but this might just be one area of the school system where a central lead would be welcomed.

5. Charitable foundations

Look carefully in their small print and you'll find that Oxford University Press (OUP) is a charity, making handsome profits from schools. Might the Masters and Scholars of the Ancient University step forward and carry, free of charge to schools, primary teaching vacancies on OUP's well established website, currently frequented by thousands of teachers? Could the respected Education Endowment Foundation (EEF), National Foundation for Education Research (NFER) or Education Development Trust (formerly CfBT) devote some of their resources to subsidise online recruitment of school leaders? Other educational publishers or charitable foundations may be willing and equipped to take on such an initiative.

****

Across the kingdom, schools individually, in primary-secondary clusters, in MATs, in all kinds of partnership and alliances are engaged in a wide range of 'grow your own' strategies to bring on the next generation of teachers and leaders. That's as it should be. But there are few schools during the interview seasons which are not having to pay over precious funds to a profit-making company in order to be fully staffed for the start of each term.

Resources are precious and becoming ever more so. We need to do things differently. There *must* be an adventurer or two out there who can make this happen. It would be financially transformational for schools.

INNOVATION = AMBITION + CHANGE + DELIVERY

A defining characteristic of our age is that the extraordinary becomes the commonplace, at a faster and faster rate. The near horizon is being transformed before our eyes.

The tech FAANGs – Facebook, Apple, Amazon, Netflix and Google – are busy shaping our lifestyles: from drones delivering grocery orders into smart homes to driverless cars being tested on the medieval streets of Oxford and Cambridge; from Saudi Arabia's new vision of the dreamers' city of Neom on the edge of the Red Sea to 3D photocopiers replacing traditional surgery.

Underpinning this phenomenon of the extraordinary becoming the everyday lies human invention in a teeming world of more than seven billion people, interconnected through social media in a fashion humankind has never before experienced.

'Innovation' is defined in the Oxford English Dictionary as 'the alteration of something established'. In the context of educational leadership and policy making, I see this formula operating: Innovation = Ambition + Change + Delivery. In practice, leaders in the education business are acutely aware of these three constituent and dynamic parts.

Good intentions are laudable, but not enough.

Ambition

Achieving excellence in any sphere of public life is rooted in leaders *caring* more than others think is wise and *risking* more than others think is safe. Further, excellence is rooted in leaders *dreaming* more than others think is practical and *expecting* more than others think is possible.

These ambitions to improve upon previous best have of course to be tempered by context and culture. Ambitions need to be skilfully shared by leaders and policy makers so that 'followers' share the same ambitions.

Clarity is paramount, matched by timely communication. We can all think of good decisions failing to be implemented because they were poorly communicated. Sadly, poor decisions, well communicated, can find their way into practice.

In education settings today – in schools, colleges and universities – true ambition is about realising a step change in outcomes for young people entering a global community and market-place. Students in the 21st century are destined through their working lives to move within and between countries with a frequency undreamt of in previous generations.

Change

Questing to achieve world-class excellence demands a hearts and minds commitment amongst all stakeholders to embrace change. Respectful leaders, from primary headteachers to local authority directors of education, in large part determine that climate. Shrewd policy makers recognise that a cardinal feature of change is that some people will misunderstand or misinterpret what is being proposed. Some will be inclined to build walls, while others will build windmills and become key personnel in effecting improvement.

Developing capacity in senior staff entails climbing inside their skin and genuinely listening. Staff need reassuring that while *change* is permanent, individual changes are not to be perceived as negating historic and valued ways of working.

Leaders regularly talk about 'stuff happens' and the unintended consequences of legislation. The wisest amongst them remind us that education reform is a people business in which, following a crucial piece of communication, the recipients will observe: 'I don't remember exactly what you said. I do remember how you made me feel.'

Delivery

First, leaders and policy makers need to create a 'we' not an 'I' culture. They must set out to see the best in people, dwell on the positive, acknowledge and applaud success, while at the same time being focused on rooting out obstacles which delay desired outcomes.

Second, leadership at all levels needs to place great store by how well it can create 'a sense of urgency at the right time' and a shared 'it's never too late' mentality amongst teams of colleagues. Thoughtful and convincing leadership recognises that not everything can be achieved at the same time, but that colleagues can 'shift gear' for a sustained period of time if there is the collective ambition to transform and innovate.

Third, leaders should look *inwards* in their organisations in order to secure wise and tested ideas; and *outwards* to seize innovation which can be shaped in the best interests of students and staff. Great design lies in stitching together the best practice from within and outside the organisation.

Fourth, those with final executive responsibilities must value 'soft power': the ability to achieve influence by building networks and communicating compelling narratives. And they must, as ambassadors for reform, thrive on and enjoy balancing professional autonomy and sharp accountability.

****

Few education leaders would claim to be innovators in the mould of Steve Jobs, Sheryl Sandberg and James Dyson.

But they might well argue that within their own settings and institutions they are often seeking to alter something established. They are questioning orthodoxies and driving change to ensure improved social, physical and intellectual outcomes for young people.

The 19th century English poet Percy Bysshe Shelley described poets as 'the unacknowledged legislators of the world'. Many years working in the education system tell me rather that *teachers* are the real unacknowledged legislators.

Theirs is a decisive influence upon the predispositions and habits of early years' children, the formative skills and knowledge of primary pupils, the academic and vocational pathways of secondary aged students, the attitudes and expectations of the next generation of teachers in training, the research interests of university students.

The future comes upon us ever faster. We search for a language to describe a screen-obsessed world. What remains a truism is that no school, college, university or education system can in the end be better than the quality and innovative thinking of its teaching force. Policy makers and leaders ignore this fact at their peril.

SHAPING THE NATIONAL STANDARDS OF EXCELLENCE FOR HEADTEACHERS

(see page 139)

When reflecting on the great schools globally I have visited, I see schools which excel at what they do in a consistent manner; they have strong values and high expectations; their achievements do not happen by chance but through reflective, carefully planned strategies; there is a high degree of internal consistency; and leadership is well distributed and ambitious to move forward.

In summary, excellence is not an act, but a habit. The staff practise being excellent. What then is the starting point for inspirational schools and leadership?

First, it is knowing where you want to go. At the heart of that knowledge is deciding what it is that you want your children and students to have by way of 21st century minds, knowledge and skills. Great school leaders have thought through this question very carefully and of course are prepared to adapt as they proceed.

Second, these leaders decide, with their colleagues, what the curriculum should be and how it should be organised. After all, what we teach lies at the heart of every school. Schools embody continuity, tradition, constancy in a changing world. Schools in any culture seek to balance the transmission of values from the past with anticipation of future cultural norms.

The international architect Richard Rogers argues compellingly: 'Architecture is measured against the past, you build in the present and you try to imagine the future'. So too with schools. They are immutably of the past, present and the future, and what they choose to teach their children is a similar blend of history, contemporary knowledge and a skill-set for today and tomorrow.

The National Standards of Excellence for Headteachers are designed to inspire public confidence in today's and tomorrow's headteachers. They list 24 characteristics expected of those who lead schools, and against which headteachers and principals can benchmark their professionalism.

In any survey of which professions are trusted most by the general public, primary and secondary headteachers regularly appear in the top few positions. This is nothing new, but in an era when professions are properly under increased scrutiny, the content of the new Standards afford an opportunity to reaffirm the vital roles of school leaders.

Expectations of what professionals can and should achieve rise inexorably. Think for a moment what we expect today of our architects, our doctors, our engineers, our pilots. Headteachers today, in order to inspire public confidence, require a tremendous breadth of knowledge and range of skills, not to mention highly developed inter-personal qualities.

In the modern age when change is a constant, especially fuelled by instant messaging and social media, raising aspirations in young people is naturally expected – by parents, by politicians, by media commentators. Schools and school leaders are under the microscope of published examination results, expected to produce year-on-year improvements and provide those many extras in a child's education.

Further, in a rich society there are proper concerns that wealth and opportunity are unevenly spread. Schools are rightly seen as places which can make a tangible difference in closing achievement gaps. This can only be done with inspired teaching and an innovative curriculum offer

Strong leadership thrives confidently on accountability and does not see it as an intrusion or obstacle. Inspiring leaders embrace opportunities to be 'entrepreneurial and innovative' where there are evident gains for staff development and for enhancing pupils' experiences within and outside the school.

Capturing much of the above, the National Standards are organised in four *domains:*

1. Qualities and knowledge

Unsurprisingly in this domain, characteristics to be found in teachers and headteachers alike are included: working with moral purpose, demonstrating optimistic personal behaviour, drawing on their own scholarship.

The added leadership dimension comes with an expectation that headteachers will communicate a compelling vision to their school community and empower pupils and staff alike to excel in their work. To do this, they need to have a wise understanding of how to translate national policy into a given context, being aware too of what the best global systems of education provide.

2. Pupils and staff

The well-being and achievements of staff and pupils lie at the heart of this domain, with the clear recognition that no school and no classroom can be better than those who lead and teach within them. Headteachers are urged to ensure that equality is advanced, pupil disadvantage combatted, and the best classroom practice is shared between staff. Accountability, professional conduct and the spotting of emerging talents are underpinning themes.

3. Systems and process

It is the stuff of leadership manuals that attention to detail with systems and organisation matters. This domain thus ranges across wise financial management, performance management and robust governance. It is equally focused on the proper safeguarding of pupils and developing their exemplary behaviour in school and in the wider community. Distributed leadership are two watchwords.

4. The self-improving school system

Within this fourth domain lie the most exciting strands for current and future school leaders: to create outward-facing schools; to challenge educational orthodoxies in the best interests of the students they serve; to shape the future of the teaching profession; and to model entrepreneurial and innovative approaches to school improvement and leadership.

That is some agenda.

The four domains of the Standards add up to an ambitious and motivating set of statements. They are underpinned by a belief in the fundamental importance of lifelong education, securely rooted in what young people experience during their school days. The National Standards are a clarion call to inspire current and future generations of great school leaders who practise excellence as a habit.

EDWARD BEAR SYNDROME

'Here is Edward Bear, coming downstairs now, bump, bump, bump, on the back of his head, behind Christopher Robin. It is, as far as he knows, the only way of coming downstairs, but sometimes he feels that there really is another way, if only he could stop bumping for a moment and think of it. And then he feels that perhaps there isn't.'

Winnie-the-Pooh. A.A. Milne

Over the past 20 years, the school system in England has improved beyond recognition.

Yet there remain too many schools which just bob along, never quite breaking through to becoming thriving and confident communities. They survive and falter, rather than flourish. They fail to reach that 'tipping point' which leads to sustaining success. When ill winds blow, their leaders rush to build walls rather than windmills. They dig deep in their routines to find reasons not to change.

So what's to be done?

What needs to happen *differently* to effect lasting change in these faltering schools, in the best interests of pupils and staff? Leaders might consider this 'less is more' blueprint for school self-improvement: seven platforms upon which to build success.

Platform 1: Expectations

Establishing whole-school high expectations is the starting point for any improvement journey. This starts with those who govern and lead the school. Context matters, so a locally determined set of 'non-negotiables' must be agreed by all those who work and study within the particular school community. An agreed set of 'living values' underpins a healthy organisation.

Consistency of expectations in classrooms, corridors, recreational spaces, staffroom and offices is a watchword. Collusion with any unsatisfactory practice is unacceptable. Sameness is the enemy of good. Individuality and difference should be valued.

Platform 2: Behaviours

The behaviour of staff, students and families towards one another and the school must at all times be proper. Young and old, male and female alike are treated with dignity. Clear examples of best behaviours and attitudes are modelled consistently and shared. There is no shouting or 'dark sarcasm of the classroom'. There is laughter and kindness.

From the moment anyone comes through the school entrance they know which kinds of behaviour are acceptable, and those which are not. Staff are expected to be professionally *friendly* towards one another, but not *friends* who bring into school issues which should be left at the school-gate. A professional working environment permeates.

Platform 3: Environments

School environments shape lives and determine staff and students' daily well-being. Governors and leaders must establish consistently safe, clean and engaging learning environments, from classrooms to corridors to playgrounds to the wider campus. If the tiniest piece of glass is cracked or graffiti appears, prompt action for renewal must be taken. The right temperature and degree of light for high quality learning should be the norm.

Dining facilities, library spaces, staff workrooms, staff and student common rooms – attention to detail in these spaces lifts morale and the 'can-do' spirit of everyone. Create an environment – every nook and cranny – which lifts the spirits, and everyone's attendance rates will rise.

Platform 4: Teachers

Teachers determine pupils' outcomes; no school can be better than the quality of its teachers. The recruitment and retention of high quality teachers is fundamental. The forging of a cadre of colleagues who promote a love of learning, scholarship and creativity amongst their pupils is well on the way to producing a thriving school. Teachers should know their subjects and shape a vibrant curriculum. Investment in their professional development is a critical aspect of a school which is intent on building success.

All teachers should be well educated and well read. Where teachers require an update in their skills and knowledge, the school's obligation is to provide proper support, and hold teachers to account. Above all, the teaching staff must have challenging ambitions for all students that they can attain high outcomes, academically and socially.

Platform 5: Supporters

'Supporters' are many and varied in the school context. In-class support staff are expected to make a significant contribution to pupils' learning and progress; their professional development is as vital as that provided for teachers. School administrators create ways of doing which ensure day-to-day organisation is consistently smooth and enabling.

Families are actively engaged in their children's learning, and communication with them is first-class. Governors play a vital part in keeping the school on its toes, regularly and without flinching from difficult decisions. The skills of key community partners are harnessed for students' well-being and readiness for transition to the next phase of their education.

Platform 6: Leaders

Think of children and young people first as leaders: harness their distinctive knowledge to shape the school's present and future successes. All staff should be aware that 'leadership' in one guise or another is expected of them and that the school believes in growing its own leadership teams. Current and potential middle and senior leaders need strong professional support and development, and clear lines of accountability. They need to see the enjoyment, fun and job satisfaction there is to be had in a leadership position.

Headteachers remain decisive in moving a school forwards at pace, ambitious for success, restless to improve. They need to take the right advice, and ignore the wrong advice. They need to recognise and seize the 'tipping points' – and demonstrate that it's a great job to lead a school.

Platform 7: Critics

On a journey of school improvement, there will be welcome and unwelcome critics. Leaders need to see their school from time to time through the eyes of the complaining customer. Interpret and harness that complaint well, and fewer complaints will come in the future. Schools need to be unrelenting in how they manage community perceptions of what they are doing. Reputations are hard won, and too easily lost.

The increasingly successful school welcomes critical friends to visit and report on what is going well and what still needs improvement. It certainly has no qualms about *leading* a passing inspection or review team to catch staff and students at their best.

TWO MINUTE LEADERSHIP

A celebrated French general was once tactlessly asked, after a famous victory, if it hadn't really been won by the second-in-command.

The general thought for some time before answering: 'Maybe so. But one thing is certain. If the battle had been lost, I would have lost it'.

As a deputy head I vividly recall being told by my headteacher that I would not make the mistakes I was watching him make – but that I should proceed with my career in the certain knowledge that I would make my own. His advice was perspicacious.

Leaders are primates and human, prone to wise judgement and crass error in equal measure. There is just no stopping it. But there is something to be learned from observing others, both what they do successfully and where they falter. In that spirit, and in the spirit of those one-minute-manager and one-minute-father books you find in any airport bookshop, the following are offered.

Rooted in various encounters, they are not presented in any order of importance, rather as a series of take-away moments. There is space at the end of the list for you to add your own, to pass on to those with whom you work and who are busy noting your mistakes ….

- *Talk with and listen to the students* – they help you keep your finger on the school's pulse, its corridor rumour and playground gossip. Walk through classrooms every day you can, even if it's just to say 'hello'.

- *Know your community* – if it is changing, respond promptly. Don't wait to be told that the number of bilingual learners has doubled since you last walked the corridors.

- *Compliment someone at least once a day* – you may find it hard to include all your staff here, but try. Practise on someone who might least expect the smile from you. Offer to take a lesson for them. And remember: cynics don't only grow old, they die.

- *Be resilient in the face of failure* – admit when you're wrong. When you apologise, never add 'but' to the end of the apology or you'll gain a reputation for insincerity.

- *Grasp nettles tightly* – then they won't hurt. Remember Aesop? Spot the member of staff who has retired, but hasn't told you yet.

- *Remember Bertrand Russell* – 'the trouble with the world is that the stupid are cocksure and the intelligent are full of doubt'.

- *Invest in high quality toilets for students* – you won't regret explaining that additional expenditure to the governors. They have children at the school, and will have been told about the plush soap dispensers, luxuriant plants and framed mirrors in the loos.

- *Invest in classrooms* – teachers and students spend 1500 hours a year in them. Buy a chaise longue, Nespresso machine, iPad and water cooler for every teacher.

- *Abolish bells* – they belong in another era. Put plants and carpets across the curriculum. Install a luxury fish tank in the entrance foyer to calm irate parents.

- *Your best friends are the dustbin and the delete button* – so much 'stuff' comes your way, so protect others from it. Cut bureaucracy for your colleagues. De-clutter classrooms, offices and staffroom – secure a deal with a skip company.

- *Less is more – be concise*: the Lord's Prayer – 54 words. The Ten Commandments – 297 words. The American Declaration of Independence – 300 words. The EEC Directive for exporting duck eggs – 26,911 words.

- *Bottle the teachers who are young at heart* – infect everyone with their talents. Ensure a variety of skills and intelligences in staff you appoint. Grow your own great people. Certainly look to recruit people who are brighter than you are.

- *Stick close to your values* – and be occasionally sceptical of them. Be explicit about the ethical principles upon which you lead.

- *Have confidence in your moral commitment, instinct and intuitions* – and have someone to restrain you, probably matron or the groundsman.

- *Enjoy confronting authority and taking risks* – practise the Jesuit principle of management, namely that it's easier to beg forgiveness than seek permission. Say 'no' to a directive and that you believe instead in phyletic gradualism.

- *Thrive on accountability* – and occasional chaos. Remember the old maxim (misquoting Kipling) that if you have kept your head when everyone around you is losing theirs, you probably haven't quite understood what's going on.

- *Keep in mind the big picture* – someone has to. Remember the 'third eye' – challenge orthodoxies even if you then find out why some things are orthodox; it's worth the journey.

- *Communicate, communicate, communicate* – and time the communications well. Timing is all. If colleagues disagree with you, they'll say you haven't been communicating properly. How you say something is as important as what you say.

- *Tell good stories* – people remember them. Stories define who you are in the minds of others, for better or worse. Humour works, not sarcasm.

- *Avoid delusions of grandeur* – for everyone's sake, be reasonably predictable. Perception is all. You're paid handsomely to smile. And be a great teacher!

- *Don't assume rationality on the part of the people you are dealing with* – accept the idea that there are multiple perceptions of every situation. Learn to live with shades of grey.

- *Spare a thought for Bloom* – knowledge, comprehension, application, analysis, evaluation, synthesis. Not everyone is as capable as you pretend to be of moving upwards through Bloom's taxonomy of thinking. Some will get stuck half-way.

- *Pace yourself* – excellence is not an act but a habit. Focus on a limited number of objectives at a time. Secure a culture of co-workers, not hierarchies.

- *Read Seneca and the Stoics* – strive for moral and intellectual perfection. Get the staff to read widely. Be curious and find time for your own interests. Ditch the guilt.

- *Take Tuesdays off* – if you're going to take 'dedicated headteacher time' off-site, don't do it on a Friday or the staff will think you're off to the ski slopes for the weekend. Learn to develop your inner sloth. Rest your heartbeat somehow.

- Add your own.....

TEACHING

'Teaching and learning are a great double act. One requires the other.'

'Great lessons are all about richness of task, rooted in teachers' excellent subject knowledge and passion to share that wisdom with students.'

'For most mortals, acquiring a new skill is a mix of perspiration, repetition, frustration, humour and memorable lightbulb moments.'

'When record-breakers in any walk of life achieve a new record, their starting point is an unshakeable belief that they *can* do it. Great teachers engender that same self-belief in their students: difficulty is both pleasurable and the starting point for mastery and true scholarship.'

LIFELONG LEARNING: IN PRAISE OF THE TEACHER

Through 40 years of teaching I have greatly enjoyed watching students learn. And I pride myself on being a fair teacher of all ages.

Early teaching days in Brixton classrooms, an untrained graduate with a degree in linguistics, I well recall helping primary and secondary children newly arrived in London with their basic command of English.

I watched in wonder how quickly they absorbed the grammar, syntax and vocabulary I modelled for them and how enthusiastically they practised in class and at home. Many of the youngsters asked for extra copies of the worksheets, so they could in turn teach their parents. That was my day job in the mid-1970s.

As a young impecunious teacher, three evenings a week I also taught English to adults. My classes were a fascinating mix of Russian émigrés, Spanish/Italian au pairs, and first generation immigrants from the Indian sub-continent. Their passion to master English was humbling, a mastery they viewed as the golden key to a flourishing life in British society and good job prospects in the capital city.

I mention these formative language teaching experiences because, working in the Gulf countries over the past year, I have started learning Arabic, from square one.

I have the great good fortune to enjoy one-to-one tuition with a gifted Tunisian teacher who is also a highly skilled translator. His knowledge of different forms of Arabic – from Algeria to Egypt to Oman to Saudi – is formidable. He shares with me dialect, slang and vocabulary from across the Levant and Gulf. And we speak French together for fun and occasional clarification. I hold his tri-lingualism in awe.

It would be fair to say that this experience of new learning has been pleasurable and painful in equal measure.

As a boy my parents sent me to France to learn a modern foreign language. I absorbed it rapidly, living with a family in Bordeaux who fortunately spoke no English and in an era when English was not the lingua franca of youth that it is today. My fluency in French is rooted in those immersive teenage years.

Learning Arabic aged 64 is quite a different experience. It's tough, very tough.

There are moments during Friday afternoon sessions when my brain truly hurts. I have to ask the tutor to pause while my ageing synapses sort themselves out. The lessons are oral and aural. Everyday expressions, singulars and plurals, conjugations, masculine and feminine nouns and adjectives which shape Arabic – they come at me with an intensity and speed which I love yet find difficult to process.

The tuition is exceptional, resources tailor-made, the orchestration of language building impeccable. I try to do my homework a couple of evenings a week, supported by YouTube videos which assist with pronunciation. I practise my Arabic letter writing and, while driving, spot number plates and posters for reinforcement. I listen keenly while in meetings conducted in Arabic and, on good days, pick out enough words and phrases to get a sense of what is being said.

My wife is taking evening classes with a different tutor. Thus we have magnetic Arabic numbers and letters on the fridge. We have words in Arabic script posted around the flat to reinforce our weekly lessons.

Yet my learning is hesitant. Progress is much slower than that of the children and young adults I taught in the 1970s, new to the UK and the English language. Lifelong learning is a mantra I have long promoted; in practice, it is proving a serious challenge.

Professionally, I have again this year had the privilege of being in hundreds of classrooms: from kindergarten to university tutorials, in public, private and international schools and institutes. Naturally I have seen teaching of varying degrees of effectiveness. But I have rarely seen a teacher who doesn't have an enthusiasm to impart new learning to their students.

As the academic year draws to a close, students counting down the days, let us pause to applaud teachers everywhere. Their passion, skills, knowledge and sheer resilience make a real difference to learners in classrooms.

For most young students I hazard the view that the school year may have had its ups and downs, but that at term end they can look back on much that has been achieved. As an older learner, I look back on my achievements in Arabic and feel less certain. I shall of course persist with this enchanting language, inshallah, ever encouraged by my outstanding tutor.

THE TEACHERS' STANDARDS: WHY THEY MATTER

(see page 131)

September 2012 sees the introduction of new Teachers' Standards, which replace the existing qualified teacher status (QTS) and core standards, and the GTCE's Code of Practice for Registered Teachers in England. The new standards set out the minimum requirements for teachers' professional practice and conduct. Teachers' performance is to be assessed against them as part of the new appraisal arrangements for schools.

In drawing up the standards during 2011, the Review's remit was to develop new standards of competence, ethics and behaviour that reflect the trust and professionalism society should expect from its teachers. To that end, the new Standards begin with a preamble, a founding statement of expectations:

Teachers make the education of their pupils their highest concern, and are accountable for achieving the highest possible standards in work and conduct. Teachers act with honesty and integrity; have strong subject knowledge, keep their knowledge and skills as teachers up-to-date and are self-critical; forge positive professional relationships; and work with parents in the best interest of their pupils.

The Review considered a wide range of international and national evidence, including examples of teachers' standards from other countries and how they are used. We felt that the new standards had to provide a strong benchmark of the minimum requirements that should be expected of trainees and teachers.

In essence, the standards had to raise the bar and highlight the characteristics of good teaching. Above all, the standards needed to be clear, simple and assessable; to identify the key elements of teaching; and set out the expectations of professional conduct that underpin the practice of teachers at all career stages.

We were clear, however, that the standards should not define the award of QTS and the end of a teacher's induction period as two separate career stages, principally because the induction period should be about consolidating ITT and demonstrating consistency of practice. Trainees and teachers should demonstrate that they meet all the standards, which define the level of practice at which all qualified teachers should be expected to perform.

The new standards do not prescribe in detail what good or outstanding teaching looks like; this should be determined by ITT providers, headteachers and teachers using their professional judgement as relevant to context, roles and responsibilities. The new standards should assist them in making such decisions by providing a clear framework within which such judgements can be made.

The Review also recommended that the Post-Threshold, Excellent Teacher and Advanced Skills Teacher Standards should be discontinued, and advocated the introduction of a Master Teacher Standard *(see page 135)*. This Standard is made up of five core domains (modelled on international best practice) within which very good teachers can demonstrate their abilities:

1. Knowledge

2. Classroom performance

3. Pupil outcomes

4. Environment and Ethos

5. Professional Context

It is the Review group's view that the new Teachers' Standards, and the proposed Master Teacher Standard, will provide a new progressive career framework for teachers that will both raise the prestige of the profession, and improve teacher quality.

In my view, the 2012 Teachers' Standards are a once-in-a-generation opportunity for teachers across the country to unite behind a set of professional expectations that are focused unequivocally on the classroom. If all teachers meet these expectations we shall have a profession of which society can be rightly proud.

VISIBLE IMPROVEMENTS

'How can I demonstrate visible improvements when an observer or an inspector comes into my class and asks the pupils what they are doing?'

I have observed over 8000 lessons in the past decade, entering classrooms as an inspector, a reviewer/Blinker, a coach in primary, special and secondary schools – from Mumbai to New York, Barcelona to Birmingham, Jeddah to Jarrow. And the recurring question from UK teachers is the one above.

The Ofsted inspection framework places a strong emphasis on key skills in primary and secondary schools. The definition of outstanding teaching makes explicit that the teaching of reading, writing, communication and mathematics must be 'highly effective and cohesively planned and implemented'.

The same emphasis features in the Teachers' Standards. All teachers must have a clear understanding of appropriate teaching strategies for early reading and mathematics. Equally, teachers of whatever age range or subject are expected to promote 'high standards of literacy, articulacy and the correct use of standard English'. These are not easy demands for teachers.

TeachersMedia have produced a short series of 20-minute programmes filmed in carefully chosen primary and secondary classrooms. In the course of the series I present practical tips to teachers wanting to make sure that they can evidence pupils' progress, set in the context of excellent everyday practice.

Of the four programmes, two are based in primary schools looking at English and mathematics; and two are focused on differentiation and literacy in secondary schools. What do the films offer by way of example and advice?

Creating an exciting climate for learning

One key aspect which shines through in the films is that in exciting classrooms there is that judicious balance of the fun and fundamentals of

47

learning. Fun, humour and warm relationships abound. So too does an unequivocal focus on practising basic and higher order skills. Excellent teachers accept no substitute.

The engaging classrooms we see in the four programmes provide 'climates' for learning which engender confidence and motivation among the learners. Critically, there is no fear of failure because the teachers and pupils alike support one another's triumphs and disasters. Opportunities for risk taking, exploration of new knowledge and concepts, and experimentation permeate. Learners' potential is spotted and encouraged. In the true sense of the word, education – 'to lead out' – underpins the learning environment.

Inspiring and vibrant teaching

At the heart of excellent progress by pupils is motivating and inspiring teaching. Ask any group of pupils, from age 7 to 17, what makes for effective classroom learning and they talk about the teacher who loves their subject and shares that passion with their students through rich tasks and activities. To use a word that has sadly gone out of fashion in some quarters, it is the promotion of *scholarship* that matters.

Pupils in these films are infected by the enthusiasms of their teachers. In my experience, pupils deeply respect the teacher who has a breadth and depth of knowledge that they themselves can, at their age, only dream of and aspire to.

Just think for a moment of the teachers you remember with affection from your own school days. Yes, it will be the teacher who knew and valued you as a person. It will also be a mathematician, a biologist, a linguist or a musician whose own memorable scholarship was not in doubt, who shared their ambitions and enthusiasms.

The vibrant classrooms we chose to feature in the series are places where what is on the walls, windows, floor and ceiling matters. The teachers have given thought to learning prompts, keywords, photos (taken by students) celebrating achievement, and displays of high quality pupils' work to which their peers can aspire.

Furthermore, book and technological resources are accessible and fit for purpose. The held-held device is present, no more nor less important than a pair of scissors. It is a tool for learning which each generation of young people masters more skilfully than the majority of its teachers.

I once asked a group of talented 14-year-olds to draw images of what made for effective and less effective lessons. Intriguingly, they set to on their sugar paper to draw a series of expanding and contracting heads. The more effective a lesson became, they charted with their colour pens, the larger the students' heads and the smaller the teacher's head. They were seeking to point out that the teacher begins the lines of enquiry, giving space for students to continue the journey.

I can think of no better image to describe what I see in the best classrooms around the world. And that journey offers to the observer, in every classroom, clear evidence of pupils' progress.

Skilful orchestration

A hallmark of the featured classrooms is that time within lessons is skilfully orchestrated, evident to the live observer but not always the easiest aspect of practice for a camera to capture.

The teachers do not rattle on at pace, galloping through the scheme of work for fear of running out of time. Rather, they deliver narratives and explanations at a speed consistent with pupils' understanding and internalising new concepts, knowledge and skills. It means that the films capture young minds reflecting, pondering and being challenged as they tackle a demanding activity – and that represents manifest good progress by pupils.

Teaching and learning are a great double act. One requires the other. The effective teacher helps pupils, through various techniques, to think about the progress they are making: daily, weekly, and over a term or a year.

The teacher and pupil reflecting on progress together, through marking and dialogue, identify next steps in learning and what particular support or extension might be required to ensure the pupil's individual needs are met. This is as true of an infant teacher observing the development of fine motor skills, as it is of the GCSE history teacher concentrating on improving essay writing skills with their group.

In the same way that a hand surgeon needs to have detailed knowledge of the nerves, tendons and arteries of that part of the body, so the professional teacher needs excellent technical background know-how. The primary specialist has a clear understanding of cognitive development in seven-year-olds, and how teaching approaches need to be adjusted to secure positive progress in mathematics in a Year 2 classroom. Equally, the A-level teacher of economics brings to their seminar group a secure command of the impact of different study skills and analytics, so that students can approach a demanding concept from different directions in order to grasp its complexities.

Talk less, do less

Best practice for encouraging pupil progress in these filmed classrooms is certainly rooted in the teacher who expects, from time to time, to talk and do less than her students. A Year 11 mathematics teacher explains how, in the course of the following week and sharing her lesson plans with students, one pair will lead the lesson starter, another will lead the mini-plenary, how yet another will conclude the lesson.

To teach is to learn, and the best teachers enable their pupils to make visible improvements by doing just that on a regular, well planned basis.

Consistent with the age and growing maturity of the pupil, creative teachers encourage independence. This independence is demonstrated by pupils taking a responsible and conscientious approach to their classwork and homework. It will not happen by magic. Effective teachers nudge, cajole and model independent learning habits. In common with good parents, they give 'roots and wings' to children.

The best lessons

As the presenter of these TeachersMedia programmes, and knowing from the inside the qualities of each of the featured schools, I hope viewers may learn more than the many specific tips about demonstrable pupil progress in literacy, mathematics and differentiation. These schools also show what it means to create 'sparkling classrooms':

- great lessons are all about richness of task, rooted in teachers' excellent subject knowledge and passion to share that wisdom with students
- pupils' prior knowledge of a subject is endlessly surprising

- timely digression and intervention promote memorable learning moments
- high quality marking from teachers fuels pupils' rapid progress
- doing more of the same does not transform standards of attainment – doing *differently* can
- the best teachers are children at heart
- observing the best lessons, you just don't want them to end.

It was said of Sir Christopher Wren: 'If you seek his monument, look around you.' Confident teachers in vibrant classrooms can invite, with confidence, any passing observer to see the cocktail of pupils' progress right across their classrooms: from detailed record-keeping and regular, incisive marking to the quality of their wall displays, oral interventions and the passion they bring to a subject.

DIFFICULTY IS PLEASURABLE

When I assert to audiences of teachers that we need to make children 'cry intellectually' once a week, they frequently look askance. Perhaps 'wobble mentally' is a kinder way of putting it, though that risks softening my argument.

What I am suggesting, with a degree of provocation and a wish to challenge a few classroom orthodoxies, is that learning in any context is frequently most fun when the learner is pushed to her or his limits. Think of a Year 6 pupil wrestling with the metaphors in Ted Hughes's 'The Thought Fox', or a Year 11 student seeking to understand how an E. coli bacterium performs differently from a sub-atomic particle when observed under a microscope in a laboratory.

Think for a moment of a skill you have mastered in adult life. It might be salsa, kayaking, plumbing or jewellery making. There are always some people who, as my mother puts it, are to the manner born. They show a natural aptitude for something, and learning comes quickly and easily. But for most mortals, acquiring a new skill is a mix of perspiration, repetition, frustration, humour and memorable lightbulb moments.

In the PE context we frequently see training sessions which work students to the point of near exhaustion, to build physical stamina and to master a particular technique. But are teachers – in a risk-averse age – wary of pushing the same students to the point of intellectual exhaustion in the maths or history classroom?

A great teacher I know says that when a 10-year-old in her class makes a mental maths error, she asserts an instant 'wrong'. At times she is moved to say 'wise mistake', echoing the Apple guru Steve Jobs who always encouraged his staff to fail wisely. She affirms further that the brighter the child, the sharper will be her 'wrong'. Years of inspirational practice tell her that children don't want to hear false praise or be asked to turn yet again to a talk partner when they make a number error. The child wants to fathom it out, get a similar question right next time, and the time after that.

There are not enough teachers who subscribe to the 'difficulty is pleasurable' principle. Of course I am not advocating placing undue pressure on pupils which serves only to switch them off learning. Surely gone are such experiences as I had in a Bath primary school in the 1960s where you were told to jump into the deep pool and 'swim'. I can feel the fear to this day, and that particular instruction delayed my own basic mastery of swimming until my late teens.

A welcome feature of most classrooms I visit in this country and around the world is that teachers know their pupils well; they know pupils' interests, abilities, aptitudes and learning dispositions. They certainly know which pupils can be taken that extra intellectual mile. And yet, teachers fail sometimes to seize opportunities to move a mathematical or linguistic or geographical concept to a point where pupils are left wondering, even momentarily lost.

In memorable lessons, teachers of whatever age classes set out to ensure that at least once or twice in a session the pupils are quietly in awe of the teacher's own scholarship. Pupils are stirred to reflect: 'How did she know that? How did he work that out? That's difficult, and I want to be able to do that.'

And the skilled teacher, like the practised stand-up comic judging how long to keep his audience on hold, will then intervene with an inventive clue or comment or question to enable the pupils to share her knowledge and skills. The penny drops. The 'aha' moment of breakthrough comprehension happens. The pleasure on their faces at the difficulty surmounted is palpable.

When record-breakers in any walk of life achieve a new record, their starting point is an unshakeable belief that they *can* do it. Great teachers engender that same self-belief in their students: difficulty is both pleasurable and the starting point for mastery and true scholarship.

10,000 HOURS: WHAT MAKES A GREAT TEACHER?

Thomas More: Why not be a teacher? You'd be a fine teacher, perhaps a great one.

Richard Rich: If I was, who would know it?

Thomas More: You, your pupils, your friends, God. Not a bad public, that.

Robert Bolt: 'A Man for All Seasons'

What makes anyone accomplished at anything? Influential psychologist Anders Ericsson and polemicist Malcolm Gladwell tell us that 10,000 hours of *purposeful practice* are necessary to create real proficiency – and maybe the platform for stand-out excellence.

Think The Silver Beatles playing the clubs of Hamburg; Lewis Hamilton, aged six, driving go-karts; the young Venus Williams on Palm Beach tennis courts; Bill Gates or Steve Jobs in their formative 'garage years' – each driven by different motives, investing hours and hours to perfect what later became their greatness.

Take a regular classroom teacher, teaching upwards of 1,000 lessons a year. That's 10,000 in a decade. At a careful estimate, over several decades I have taught about 30,000 sessions to learners of all ages. And in various guises, I have been an 'observer' in just on 10,000 classrooms during the past 15 years.

What do I experience when I am in the presence of an accomplished teacher, irrespective of context and location: from Newcastle to New York, Geneva to Pune, Riyadh to Kuala Belait? Reflecting on vivid examples, I identify 10 prevalent features in the cocktail, variously distilled.

1. *Knowledge.* No teacher can survive without the fount of knowledge which lies at the core of their everyday practice. Good teachers have an innate generosity to want to share what they know. For the skilled

early years' practitioner, that knowledge lies in a deep understanding of how young children grow, and how best to intervene or draw back when children are developing their independent learning habits. For the teacher of an IB French class studying Albert Camus, it is the teacher's facility to cross-reference Sartre, Gide or Heidegger to open up an appreciation of existentialism.

The skilled teacher has knowledge effortlessly rising out of them like sap from a tree – and keeps learning and practising.

2. *Craft.* In many walks of life a 'craftsman' is revered for her or his well-honed skills, whether cooking, sculpting or operating medically. The craft of the classroom involves its own special blend: skilled configuration of the classroom and management of pupils; time creatively orchestrated; 'less is more' lesson planning; judicious harnessing of resources; intelligent questioning and thoughtful feedback; that balance of critique and worthy praise; wise promotion of mastery, scholarship and enquiry.

The reflective practitioner commands the classroom, physically and intellectually.

3. *Passion.* Love of being in a classroom with pupils is a pre-requisite for accomplished teachers, joyfully sharing those personal and professional passions which first drew them to work in schools. To watch an enthusiastic, knowledgeable teacher embed through song and repetition an understanding of key letters and sounds in a Year 1 class is to witness enviable practice. Equally impressive is the Year 9 PE teacher, a skilled sportswoman in her own right, enabling 'sport for all and excellence for some' in a lesson on badminton forehand and backhand serves.

The passion for excellence, rooted in the teacher's own achievements, is palpable and often thrilling.

4. *Values.* In a teacher's every utterance and body language, their values about education and schooling shine through. Values reflect our sense of right and wrong and what we believe to be important to us in life. Join a teacher who is reading *The Boy in the Striped Pyjamas* with their Year 6 class; see how adroitly they field the most challenging of questions and how they support those pupils struggling emotionally with the novel's

content. Or be party to an A-level history seminar wrestling with the difference between freedom fighters and terrorists, where the teacher harnesses his considerable knowledge of Gandhi, Mandela and Guevara to present objective evidence upon which students can make a judgement.

A teacher's unambiguous set of values, embodying integrity and clear conscience, underpin memorable classroom practice.

5. *Fun.* Teaching is all about communicating to students that great double act: the fun and fundamentals of learning. Watch a gifted teacher of mathematics – with a basket of home-made, practical resources – play around with prime numbers in a Year 5 class; or that same teacher work with his non-specialist colleagues to enable them to plan confidently a session for Year 4 pupils on the Fibonacci Sequence: 0,1,1,2,3,5,8,13,21,34... Dealing in fun enables students of any age to feel confident about making mistakes, learning from them, and achieving that 'aha' moment of understanding. The fundamentals in any subject demand practice, memorisation, repetition.

The fun in learning is about teachers and students sharing humour and wit; fun is equally rooted in risk taking and digression.

6. *Creativity.* The imaginative, thinking out-of-the-box spirit lies deep in great teachers' hearts and minds. They positively embrace digression and those unplanned moments of epiphany for their students. Focus on a group of Year 8 students doing a fair test in science, when the teacher comes along and introduces a rogue substance to create intellectual confusion. Listen carefully to an EAL teacher with a group of Year 10 boys newly arrived from Serbia, harnessing Google Translate to explore the language of mathematical shapes. Creativity is an element equally at home in physics, geography or drama.

The creative teacher has a predictable unpredictability about their person.

7. *Expectations.* Show me a fine teacher who does not have the highest expectations of those they teach, wherever and whomever they are teaching. When record-breakers in any walk of life achieve a new record, their starting point is an unshakeable belief that they *can* do it. The skilled teacher knows authoritatively his pupils and can cajole, enthuse, provoke, extend as she judges: we might employ the term 'differentiation'

here. Observe a passionate teacher of English enable *every* Year 7 student to grasp the metaphors in Ted Hughes's 'The Thought Fox'; see that teacher do the same for *every* Year 11 student in her class, climbing inside the complex imagery in Sylvia Plath's 'The Bell Jar'.

What teachers expect is what they get in any classroom, in any subject and in any context.

8. *Empathy.* The ability to 'climb inside the learner's skin' is a hallmark of those teachers who live long in their pupils' memories. Great Biology teachers may well have an encyclopaedic knowledge of how an E. coli bacterium performs differently from a sub-atomic particle when observed in a laboratory. The GCSE students are perplexed, and remain so even after the second explanation – until the teacher thinks differently and tries a third explanation which approaches the problem from the learner's less experienced viewpoint. Breakthrough in understanding comes. Students of any age testify to the fact that experienced teachers can empathise with the learner's predicament, can 'connect' emotionally with them, can see that grey sometimes has its place alongside black and white.

Empathy is that vital capacity in a teacher to imagine and understand that the learner may well have a different frame of reference.

9. *Resilience.* Building learners' resilience in a contemporary world of 'snow-plough' learning devices is not to be under-estimated: 'What's a cosine?' asks the teacher. 'It's that button on the calculator,' comes the flawless answer. As vital as leading lessons with fun is the teacher's commitment to lead with intrigue: taking pupils out of their comfort zones, making learning difficult and perplexing as the moment arises. What doesn't kill you intellectually certainly makes you stronger – ask any student of Further Maths. The wise and practised teacher also recognises that their own trade is a demanding one: knowing how to pace oneself daily, weekly, termly is an art and a science in itself.

Resilience is two-track: one for the pupils' stamina in new learning; and one for the teachers' self-preservation and ultimate flourishing. Live to teach another day.

10. *X Factor.* The cocktail is more or less prepared. The distillation is incomplete without the X factor. No two teachers are the same; they may embody in many ways the nine aspects outlined above. Yet the unashamed joy of the generous teacher is that their own commanding classroom practice is, in the end, a matter of individual taste, tact and style. Each teacher has their own X factor, their unique ingredient of the pedagogical potion.

Classroom excellence becomes their habit, and their 'public' never forget the magic.

DIFFERENTIATION IS OUT. MASTERY IS THE NEW CLASSROOM BUZZWORD

Schools will witness a shift in jargon this year. Differentiation is out. Mastery is in. Mark my words.

In his memoir, *An Intelligent Person's Guide to Education*, former Eton headmaster Tony Little recounts the delightful story of workmen at the school uncovering fragments of a wall painting under some wood panelling. The images, from around 1520, are believed to be the earliest representation of a school scene in England. A banner headline from Roman scholar Quintilian crowns the scene '*Virtuo preceptoris est ingeniorum notare discrimina*', meaning 'the excellence of the teacher is to identify the difference in talents of students'. Or, in a word, differentiation.

The whole way in which classroom learning is organised and managed rests on fundamental beliefs about the learner and the learning process.

It is not just that doing things differently for different pupils relieves tedium and is more efficient as a means of instruction. It is also the fact that a key moral value is that each member of the class is an individual with her or his own rights, character, disposition to learning and level of understanding.

It's not a complex idea, but differentiation is difficult to get right. All teachers know that matching their teaching to students' various needs, aptitudes and preferred styles of learning is the key challenge in a classroom. The fact that teachers have to do this for 30 students at once makes it even more difficult. You could have an entire teaching career of purposeful practice – more than 10,000 hours – and still not quite crack it.

Different cultures treat differentiation in different ways. I remember training high school teachers in New York and being told that they 'differentiate by sending students to different rooms'.

In India I learned that deep cultural assumptions would not allow teachers to differentiate; all children must be taught the same topics in the same way at the same pace. And teaching in the Middle East I saw differentiation by gender and age; in some schools, boys are taught in morning classes, girls in the afternoon.

Recently a dose of an eastern-inspired 'mastery' has entered our schools, with the impact in maths being measured by an Education Endowment Foundation report. It's caught the attention of policy makers, and earlier this year the Department for Education flew in teachers from Shanghai to raise standards with their 'mastery' style. The Oxford University Press has also produced a paper exploring mastery in maths and how it can raise achievement. The national curriculum frameworks for English and maths are now rooted in it.

At the heart of the Chinese classroom is the teacher's unshakeable belief that all children are capable of learning anything if that learning is presented in the right way. The idea works on the basis that understanding is the result of high intention, sincere effort and intelligent execution, and that difficulty is pleasurable.

In lessons where mastery is practised, teachers ensure that at least once or twice in a session the students are in awe of the teacher's own scholarship. Pupils are encouraged to wonder how the teacher worked out a conundrum. The idea is that their interest will be piqued and they will want to be able to do it too.

The teacher – like a seasoned stand-up comic judging how long to keep his audience on hold – will then share an inventive clue, comment or question to enable the pupils to reveal their own knowledge and skills. The penny drops. The pleasure on their faces is clear.

One benefit of this approach is that it avoids the negative potential of differentiation which, if we are not careful, can lead to depressed expectations of what 'less able' pupils can achieve. Activities can be oversimplified; the challenge for deeper learning removed. The completion of the task at a lower level is the learner's modest prize.

Mastery also allows teachers to really challenge students. Many teachers in our risk-averse culture are wary of pushing students intellectually in the classroom.

An excellent teacher I know says that when the 10-year-olds in her class make a maths error, she asserts an instant 'wrong'. The brighter the child, the sharper her 'wrong' will be. At times she is moved to say 'wise mistake' – but that's as complimentary as it gets. Years of inspirational primary practice have taught her that children don't want to hear false praise or be asked to talk in pairs when they make a number error. The child wants to work it out, get a similar question right next time and the time after that.

It's a similar mindset to the world of elite sport. For example, the Olympic runner Mo Farah has said flatly that he can – and must – become better, run faster. He said it when he was unknown, and he'll probably say it after his best season. He is pursuing mastery, in the knowledge that he'll never reach it. It will always hover beyond his grasp.

The painter Paul Cezanne produced over 60 paintings and drawings of Mont St Victoire in his beloved Provence. He tackled the scene endlessly, varying colours, tints, shapes and shadows. In the words of one art critic, 'he was for ever approaching without quite reaching it.'

For most mortals anywhere in the world, acquiring a new skill is a mix of perspiration, repetition, frustration, humour and light-bulb moments. Mastery attracts precisely because it also eludes. As the school year unfolds, it will be interesting to see what teachers and students make of the new buzzword.

THE SURGEON AND THE SCALPEL

Recently clocking up 10,000 lesson observations in schools at home and abroad has made me think afresh about the so-called '10,000 hour rule', much championed by writers Daniel Levitin and Malcolm Gladwell: *Ten thousand hours of practice are required to achieve the level of mastery associated with being a world-class expert – in anything. Ten thousand hours is the magic number of greatness.*

In schools we might conclude that those who do lots of purposeful lesson observations are getting better at it all the time. But what if they are doing it with the wrong intent?

Lesson observations are most commonly carried out for the purpose of performance management and inspection. Many teachers I meet say that lesson observations *only* occur in their school when they are linked to grading of some kind. That is changing slowly, but the teaching profession is haunted by such judgemental behaviour. Micro-managing what happens in the classroom too often dents confidence and narrows opportunities for imaginative teaching.

A few years ago I lay on a surgeon's table, under local anaesthetic, to have a benign melanoma removed from my wrist. The lead surgeon began cutting precisely then passed over the scalpel to one of his juniors. Within just 20 seconds he seized it back, clearly not content with the direction of the incision. He at once offered both the junior and me some reassuring words.

It struck me then – it was in my early days of being an HMI – that my observing a lesson was of little use to the teacher if all I did was to offer some comments once the pupils had left the classroom. I would not have wanted the surgeon to let his junior go on cutting in the wrong direction, saving the feedback to later. My wrist is too precious to me for that.

Ever since that moment under the knife, formal inspection apart, I have rarely observed a lesson without interacting in some way.

In all the school reviews/*Blinks* I lead, I agree with teachers beforehand that I'll come into their classrooms and be an active assistant. I am not there to make judgements – I am there to share my considerable experience of what works in primary and secondary classrooms across the globe. I indulge myself in what might be called some 'spot coaching'. Selfishly, I'm there to enjoy myself and learn too.

Let me take a couple of examples.

- I enter a Year 5 class putting the adjectives *compliant, significant, resilient* into meaningful sentences. They are enjoying the task in talk partners, but I can see a good number have mastered this pretty quickly. I ask the teacher if I can take them in a slightly different direction, to make them wobble intellectually. I ask them to give me some sentences – *projecting* their voices and speaking to me with their eyes – where these adjectives are turned into nouns, and appropriate sentences created. The digression is quickly harnessed by the teacher and the lesson moves up a gear. I spend a little more time looking at their books, thank everyone, then move to Year 6.

- I enter a Year 12 History seminar where the teacher is drawing intriguing parallels between Mandela, Ghandi and Churchill, wrestling with how best to embed an understanding of contrasting leadership styles. I'm fascinated. The previous week I have been at the unveiling of Ghandi's statue in London's Parliament Square, and mention that the statues of all three leaders now stand in the Square. Students google, they call up photos of the statues and we find those outrageous lines of Churchill's about Ghandi: 'he ought to be lain bound hand and foot at the gates of Delhi and then trampled on by an enormous elephant.' I share my topical experience, the teacher and students are appreciative, and I settle back to listen to their discussions.

I am clear that a fundamental requirement of the self-improving school system demands a fresh approach to teachers being in one another's classrooms. We must put behind us this preoccupation with judgement. Instead, seize-the-moment, mutual coaching should be what characterises our daily practice. *Teaching with the door open* – literally or metaphorically – can be our professional clarion call. Let's show some trust.

There may well be a place for observations linked to performance management and, in common with the doctor or pilot, observations linked to ensuring teachers meet the requirements of their professional standards. But 'observations' as an everyday way of working together must be consigned to the educational dustbin. The surgeon and the scalpel should be a daily reminder.

CAN WE TEACH UNTIL WE ARE 70?

Having spent 40 years in the business I was not surprised to come across a survey in *The Telegraph* which indicated 'teachers are the happiest workers in Britain'. Teachers cited a combination of convivial colleagues, good conditions of service, understanding bosses and, above all, 'making a difference' in classrooms where there is laughter everyday and no two days are the same.

In passing, I am happy to report that – during the past month alone as a visitor to classrooms – my jackets, ties, socks and facial lines have all been commented upon, politely and trenchantly, by children. Out of the mouths of babes, ever sobering: a Reception child thought my phonics were dodgy; a seven-year-old said I looked much older than when I'd come to the school last year; and a 14-year-old was not impressed with my handwriting when I corrected her work.

Certainly life as a teacher is never boring. But can we stay fresh in what is by common consent a demanding environment? Can we teach until we are 70, if we so choose?

I pose this question in the light of a number of conversations I've held with teachers, headteachers and governors this year. All of them, in different ways, have had their eye on staying fresh in their own work, and have been thinking creatively about how to maintain a motivated staffroom.

Take David. He is coming up 50 and has been head of the English Department in a very good school for 17 years. During the course of a teaching and learning review I was running, he said: 'Do you know, I've got another 10 to 15 years leading this department? I'm not sure I can do it. What I'd really like is a year off leadership. I'd like time to just teach and refresh my own reading. What do you think?'

I thought his suggestion a sound one, and, with his permission, shared it with the headteacher. Result: from September he is doing just that, with the school protecting his leadership salary. From what I know of David, he'll enjoy the space; someone else in the department will step up to the mark and gain invaluable experience; and the school will have reinvigorated its distinguished Head of English.

Take Judy. She is headteacher of a very large urban primary school, and has been for 14 years. Of a similar age to David, some while ago she negotiated a way ahead with her enlightened governors. Every six years, she has a term's sabbatical – not unknown in other fields of education, but not yet common in schools. Judy sees herself as head of the school for another generation of children passing through. The school community has the constancy of her leadership, and the knowledge that she stays fresh as a leader.

Take Robert. He is chair of governors of a successful comprehensive school. During a leadership review at the school he asked me: 'How often should senior leaders and teachers get a sustained break from their work? What should we be setting aside in the budget to enable secondments and sabbaticals?' It's not often a chair of governors has asked me these things in the past, but maybe these very questions are being posed more regularly. They certainly need to be.

More revealingly, Robert went on to tell me how the school has recently enabled a number of long-serving, valued teachers to continue part-time, with creative pension solutions.

When Bismarck, in the 1880s, introduced into Germany his social insurance programmes, the pensionable age was set with the expectation that very few would reach it. In the 1940s our own William Beveridge was a little more generous in his planning. Today in the UK, the average life expectancy for a woman is 83.1 years and for a man 79.4 years, and our elected representatives are finding it predictably difficult to effect changes to the pension regime.

Even if a teacher doesn't enter the workplace until his late twenties, there are potentially 40-plus years in the profession ahead of him. I believe most teachers can continue to stay fresh in their work, and many want to do so. Enlightened governing bodies have smelt the coffee and are taking imaginative steps to bring periods of refreshment to those they employ.

David, Judy and Robert are no longer exceptions. From my experience in schools across the country, their stories are increasingly common. If the trend continues, teachers can remain the happiest of workers well into their senior years.

CURRICULUM

'Any national curriculum, anywhere in the world, is passing on to the next generation the nation's history, traditions and values. Equally that curriculum is preparing students for today's and tomorrow's global society with skills and knowledge the nation believes will be of value.'

'The citizens of tomorrow need to experience risk and even danger today. And nowhere better than under the safe and watchful gaze of the nation's teachers.'

'No need for Esperanto. The Tower of Babel is tumbling. English has become the global language. And, if they did but know it, native speakers of English have a glorious inheritance.'

'The best schools develop pupils' innate character through carefully designed and implemented whole-school values, through their daily ethos, through the dignity of positive relationships between adults and students, through the consistency of high expectations.'

'THE STATE OF THINGS CURRICULUM'

What should be taught and learned in schools? Try asking that question when next with a group of friends who are not teachers. The fact that everyone has been to school means everyone has a view on the subject.

The professional adventurer and Chief Scout Bear Grylls is the latest media personality to weigh in, proclaiming at the Global Education and Skills Forum in Dubai that his Eton education didn't prepare him well for adult life. (I wonder what one member of the audience, former Eton Headmaster Tony Little, said to him afterwards, given Little's deeply held commitment to a well-rounded education.)

Grylls, who seems not to have done too badly for himself, bemoaned: 'There's stuff I wish people had taught me. I wish they'd taught me how to keep fit, how to eat healthy food, how to lead a team, how to communicate with people. A bit of entrepreneurial stuff or citizenship – all this sort of stuff – a bit of tax, a bit of legal'.

I think the man does protest too much and, to make a publicity splash, rather under-estimates just how much Eton *did* teach him about keeping healthy, leadership and communication. It was Grylls of course who was previously criticised by the RNLI for leaving his then 11-year-old son alone on rocks in the sea by Abersoch in north Wales. He defended the stunt, saying it had been carefully planned, and argued that children needed to take more risks in life.

Matthew Arnold memorably observed that a good modern society can only come about when all its citizens are educated in 'the best that has been thought and said in the world'. That probably leads to the subject-based curriculum, for better or worse, with which we are all familiar today.

Any national curriculum, anywhere in the world, is passing on to the next generation the nation's history, traditions and values. Equally that curriculum is preparing students for today's and tomorrow's global society with skills and knowledge the nation believes will be of value.

Countries across the globe, regardless of wealth or political complexion, are wrestling with similar themes and tensions around the purposes of education and thus its content. In what proportion should we be teaching knowledge and skills? How do we secure the 3Rs? Is technology an opportunity or distraction? Is education for creating civilized citizens or tomorrow's workforce?

Working internationally, I frequently come across the International Baccalaureate and its well established learner profile, seeking to produce learners who are: inquirers, knowledgeable, thinkers, communicators, principled, open-minded, balanced, reflective and risk takers. This model, in theory and classroom practice, has much to commend it, from ages 5–18.

I find equal power in those primary and secondary schools which centre their curriculum around Howard Gardner's 'five minds for the future', creating learning opportunities which, over time, produce in young people: the disciplined mind; the synthesizing mind; the creating mind; the respectful mind; the ethical mind.

Last month I encountered a new state-of-the-art school which has set out its stall to operate what it calls a tri-lingual curriculum comprising Arabic, English and coding.

Looking back over the five decades I've been working in UK schools, one might reasonably conclude that when a fresh social challenge arises, the school system is expected to confront it. Perhaps that's just as it should be: 'the state of things curriculum.' Sex, drugs and rock'n'roll have often shaped curriculum content as much as Newton, Shakespeare and Hitler.

As a teacher in inner London in the 1970s, issues of race, gender and class filled our classrooms. Then the 'Aids epidemic' led to a flurry of personal and social education initiatives. Through the 1980s in Oxfordshire I recall 'multi-cultural education in mono-ethnic schools' influencing the curriculum, alongside economic awareness and industrial relations. Into the 1990s and citizenship arrived, closely followed by healthy eating in dining halls and health education lessons. The acronym duly expanded from PSE to PSHCE, via PSED.

With the advent of the 21st century, e-safety, safeguarding and LGBT awareness have influenced course content. Latterly, we have Hollywood star Orlando Bloom urging teachers to teach confidence; Sir Anthony Seldon wants happiness and empathy in classrooms; and, the circle turns, compulsory sex education (again) is pending legislation.

Last month in the Guardian, Peter Hyman, Headteacher of the pioneering School 21, wrote powerfully about what he describes as 'an engaged education':

Teachers are hungry for a more expansive education that connects pupils to the great works of our past but also the richness, variety and opportunities of the modern world. An education that is layered, ethical and deals with complexity as an antidote to the shallow, overly simplistic debates our young people often have to listen to. The best defence against extremism and illiberal democracy is an education that teaches reflection, critical thinking and questioning.

Observing the current education scene, one *Times* columnist wittily observed: 'One can't help but feel that, by the time teachers have got round to the empathy, the humility, the confidence and the rest of it, there will be hardly any time left for the quadratic equations, the acid-base reactions and the Beowolf.'

Talk to your non-teacher friends about what should be taught in schools!

'The State of Things Curriculum' will always be with us. When social ills emerge, politicians look for speedy answers, and schools are obvious places to which to turn. As teachers and school leaders we must learn to accept that *the best that has been thought and said* will always have to sit alongside the fads, fashions and social issues of the day.

MOVING IN ENGLISH CIRCLES

English, cries one group, should contain a solid grammatical preparation for the learning of Latin. English, cries another, should be the core subject. English, cry other voices, should never have been allowed into the syllabus; English is what my typists should have learned at school; English merely prepares the proletariat to understand the words of command. English, laments many a floundering novice teacher, is the most difficult subject of all to teach.

English? Responds a treble voice, I speak English don't I? My cobbers understand me. Why the heck should you have to teach me English at all?'

I.A.Gordon 'The Teaching of English'

Over the summer I asked a wise Swiss friend what he thought of Brexit. He didn't hesitate.

'You have London, the pound sterling and English. You'll never lose friends and influence.'

The capital city and coinage aside, he is so right about the primacy of our native language in a global society.

Over the past 50 years, English has spread more widely and penetrated more deeply than any other language. The British Council estimates that more than two billion people speak English, though an exact figure is hard to come by.

What is certain is that there are many more people speaking English as an additional language than as a native tongue. According to the distinguished linguist Braj Kachru this is 'a unique phenomenon in the history of language diffusion'.

Indian-born Kachru is particularly known for his description of English's three circles: the Inner Circle of the UK and the transplanted British communities of the US, Canada, Australia and New Zealand; the Outer Circle made up of largely British colonies, such as India, Malaysia and Nigeria; and the Expanding Circle, which takes in the rest of the world, including China, continental Europe and Latin America, where the ambitious see English as the key to advancement.

As people move up the ladder of prestige, and interact with English speakers everywhere, they adopt the internationally comprehensible language of today's global business, scientific and cultural exchanges. Working in the Arab World I hear its evolving vocabulary and syntax every day. Intriguingly, it is a language that is often markedly different from British and American English.

So the proof is out there everywhere. No need for Esperanto. The Tower of Babel is tumbling. English has become the global language. And, if they did but know it, native speakers of English have a glorious inheritance.

Do the British value what is so close to home? Writing in the 1940s, I. A. Gordon – quoted above – tried to capture attitudes then towards the language, particularly the assumption that if the people speak English, why then teach it in schools?

English as a discrete subject has been firmly on the school curriculum for at least a century. In 1921, George Sampson famously observed: 'Every teacher is a teacher *of* English because every teacher is a teacher *in* English'. In 1975, The Bullock Report championed 'language across the curriculum'.

And, amazing to think, it is nearly 20 years ago that David Blunkett wrote to primary heads at the start of the academic year announcing the arrival of the national literacy strategy.

Full marks then to academics, politicians and teachers. We have kept reminding ourselves of the importance of English in our classrooms, and put in place strategies to ensure linguistic mastery for students.

Yet the 2017 GCSE results indicate that at least 30% of the nation's 16-year-olds have not achieved the 'pass' level (grade 4) of competence in English Language which is now expected in an era of ever increasing expectations.

I have long maintained that the vast majority of our young people must leave school with the dignity of confident articulacy and fluent writing, so that they are ready to thrive in a contemporary global society. I guess that's a grade 5 in new money and, by the age of 18, most students should surely achieve that level.

In inner, outer and expanding circles throughout the world, the people of all nations quest to have a command of English.

Let all teachers in UK classrooms recommit themselves to being teachers *of* English. And let all children and young people be reminded of their not-to-be-taken-for-granted glorious inheritance: innate knowers of the English language.

WHAT ARE WE DOING ABOUT CHILDREN'S MENTAL HEALTH?

The Education Policy Institute (EPI) recently launched 'Children and Young People's Mental Health: Time to Deliver'. The report, expertly authored by Emily Frith, is the work of a year-long Commission of which I was a member. In essence, the publication draws attention to the postcode lottery of specialist mental health services for young people.

Across the country there is some excellent practice within NHS services, rightly prioritizing treatment at the point of need. Yet rising demand is challenging capacity: for example, in Essex the number of referrals had more than doubled in a year, from 3000 to 7000. And the cost, in human and financial terms, of late intervention is not acceptable in a wealthy democracy.

In his Foreword to the report, Rt. Hon. Norman Lamb MP – a long-time champion of the subject – draws attention to the Commission's research which uncovered a treatment gap, where specialist services are turning away one in four children referred to them by their GPs or teachers. He further highlights that it is not always possible to identify whether bespoke funding has reached frontline services.

The Commission's conclusions include a call for a *National Challenge on Children's Mental Health*. This picks up Theresa May's words in her first speech as Prime Minister: 'If you suffer from mental health problems, there's not enough help to hand.' At the heart of this challenge should be determined efforts and investment to intervene earlier, and to ensure that a wide range of health providers work more effectively with schools.

As one of the EPI Youth Reference Group members said: 'Teachers see kids five times a week and are the most likely group to notice children who are potentially at risk.'

The report devotes a powerful section to future priorities within the school system. Key amongst the priorities are:

- Evidence-based mental health training to be a part of initial and in-service training for teachers.

- A trained lead for mental health and well-being in every school, alongside a lead school governor for well-being.

- Pupil involvement in designing in-school support.

- Ofsted having regard to mental health in any inspection of a school or college.

- Mandatory high quality PSHE in all schools and colleges, with a focus on online risks and building resilience in young people to face the challenges of contemporary social media.

- The practice of making a young person leave their support service on their 18th birthday must end. Young people at university should be able to stay connected with their home CAMHS team and stay registered with their home GP if they prefer.

In launching the EPI report, Secretary of State Jeremy Hunt spoke eloquently and personally about the issue of online bullying, and how, as a parent of three young children, he was keenly aware of what parents and teachers are having to manage.

He observed that when he was a child, if you were bullied at school at least you could escape when you went home. But pernicious texting means a young person today finds it very difficult to escape – and hence he highlighted the critical role of teachers in early identification of mental health symptoms and helping children to build resilience.

Whilst a report such as this one tends by its very nature to identify problems in the system in order to make recommendations for improvement, Commissioners on their visits around the country saw many impressive projects, from Birmingham to Essex, Oxfordshire to Barnsley. Professionals leading this work must be applauded and their practices shared.

And this from Longwood Primary Academy in Harlow, devised by headteacher James Hollinsley – their PROGRESS programme which has had a decisive impact across the school on children's self-esteem and readiness to learn:

PROGRESS stands for:

1 **P**rovide a place to talk and feel protected

2 **R**aise the roof of resilience

3 **O**penly celebrate achievements

4 **G**row and nurture the family unit

5 **R**apid intervention and referral

6 **E**-safety to reduce risk

7 **S**trive to create a secure utopia

8 **S**tability and clarity in behaviour.

I started teaching in HM Prison Brixton in 1973. When I then moved to teach in a south London primary school I vowed that all my top juniors would leave me with strong self-esteem and the dignity of articulacy and literacy, as prerequisites for success at secondary school.

'Mental health' was not in my vocabulary 40 years ago. But it is rightly in the minds of students, parents and teachers today. On a personal level, being part of the Education Policy Institute Commission has served to remind me once more that children and young people cannot flourish in the school environment unless their self-esteem and readiness to learn are carefully nurtured by skilled teachers and support staff.

THE POWER OF LEARNING OUTDOORS

Courtesy of Mark Evans MBE, I spent a memorable few days in the Sharqiya desert of northern Oman.

Mark, originally a geography teacher, is an extraordinary explorer and Fellow of the Royal Geographical Society. His inspiring achievements include: a parachute assisted crossing of the Greenland Ice Cap; living for 12 months in a small tent within 500 miles of the North Pole, researching seasonal affective disorder; kayaking solo 1,700 km around the coastline of Oman.

His most recent big adventure saw him walk and ride with camels 1300 km from the south coast of Oman to Doha, a journey of 49 days across some of the most inhospitable terrain on earth. His beautifully illustrated book 'Crossing The Empty Quarter' and the lectures he gives on the experience are captivating.

Seven years ago he was appointed Executive Director of Outward Bound (OB) Oman which has rapidly emerged as one of the jewels in the global OB network. He and his team have carved out a distinguished track record of hosting international researchers into extreme climates, leadership courses for corporate leaders, bespoke skills sessions for trainee apprentices, and organising an array of field and study trips for local and international students.

The newly opened OB Centre which will now provide the location of many courses lies amidst vast, undulating sand dunes of a deep orange hue, the kind famed by such movies as 'Lawrence of Arabia'.

There is happily no mobile signal. The Centre is a splendid piece of architecture, wholly in keeping with its unique setting. Mark shows me round the buildings, caressed by the hot winds, with understandable but understated pride – he has taken seven years to realise the project, supported by generous sponsors and creative UK/Omani architects.

As we wander from outdoor teaching pods to indoor meeting rooms and accommodation areas, he affirms why he believes passionately in giving young people the desert experience:

The desert is an immensely powerful, silent yet humbling learning environment. With no technology to distract, and no doors to hide behind, young people come face to face with themselves.

Whilst the benefits of outdoor learning can sometimes be hard to quantify, something as simple as watching the sun sink slowly below the horizon, and the desert stars gradually emerge each night has as big an impact on corporate employees as it does on young people. Time stands still. They take stock, reflect on lessons learned and plan for their personal road ahead.

Listening to him, you want every youngster to enjoy this experience, just once in a school lifetime.

Looking up at a myriad of constellations few city dwellers ever glimpse, and with the desert night fast descending, we shared our various fond memories of field trips and school journeys. Needless to say, his globe-trotting significantly eclipsed my sheltered experiences.

As a teacher I have enjoyed the company and antics of students from Snowdonia to the South Downs, from Paris to the Brecon Beacons, from Butlins Minehead to just about every London museum, and not forgetting three decades of Saturday sports. Without exception, these school trips offered delight and adventure in equal measure to both students and staff. And it was rare to return to school and not comment on how the time outside the classroom had benefited most children, and some in particular.

We reflected on our brushes with disaster, some of Mark's quite frightening. In my case they have included the 14-year-old who failed to tell us she suffered from petit mal and then had a fit, falling down five flights of stairs in a Paris hotel. She was fine, mercifully. And the time I led a group of 50 inner-London pupils to stay for a week in St Malo, only to find on arrival that I had not properly secured appropriate visas for four of them. We reported each day at 6pm to the local gendarmerie!

There is no doubt that health and safety regulations have tightened the school journey screw over the years. Undaunted, enterprising teachers continue to enable young people in large numbers to benefit from learning outdoors, to experience triumph and failure and everything in between. Unquestionably, Forest School in UK primaries and secondaries has broadened the horizons of hundreds of thousands of pupils.

Mark and I pondered why formal schooling begins with rich outdoor learning in Reception but, as the years unfold, students study largely in classrooms; and, in some schools, field trips and study visits home and abroad are seen as add-ons, disruptive to the timetable. Maybe that is inevitable in an examination-led system.

Recently Her Majesty's Chief Inspector was moved to suggest that Ofsted has not helped with its tick-box approach to health and safety: 'Trying to insulate your pupils from every bump, germ, or bruise won't just drive you to distraction, it will short-change those pupils as well – limiting their opportunity to fully take advantage of the freedom of childhood, and to explore the world around them'.

Maybe these liberating words from the Chief Inspector will serve as a green light to schools and teachers who remain a little apprehensive about stepping beyond the confines of the school gates. Let us hope so.

Children around the world increasingly live, and are educated in urban settings. Their space for risk shrinks inexorably. So-called 'snowplough parents' drive them everywhere, track their every move through social media, and render spontaneous adventure more rare.

Against that backcloth, confident schools assert with pupils and parents the power of learning outdoors. Society should encourage them at every turn. The citizens of tomorrow need to experience risk and even danger today. And nowhere better than under the safe and watchful gaze of the nation's teachers.

Mark Evans: *www.outwardboundoman.com/centres* and *www.outwardboundoman.com/learning*

ARE GRAMMAR SCHOOLS WHAT WE SHOULD BE TALKING ABOUT?

At the start of an academic year in which the relative merits of grammar schools look set to be revisited, I am minded to look afresh at the 1944 Education Act, the foundation stones of our current schooling system.

In March 2014, to celebrate the seventieth anniversary of the '44 Act, I made a documentary for BBC Radio 4 titled *Government versus the Teachers*. In the course of interviewing a number of Secretaries of State for Education, past and present, one particular subject they spoke about stays with me: namely, the missed opportunities for technical education.

Shirley Williams, David Blunkett and Kenneth Baker, from different political perspectives, shared the view that the real failure of the post-war system in England lies in what might be described as the academic-vocational apartheid.

Rab Butler set out in 1944 a plan to educate secondary aged pupils in either secondary moderns, grammars or technical schools. But the 11+ has proved a political third rail to this day. When Harold Wilson championed comprehensive education as 'grammar schools for all', the thriving technical schools were buried. England's opportunity to provide high quality vocational and technical education was lost.

Historians often say that the one lesson of history is that we don't learn from history. In 1963 John Newsom and his colleagues presented to the government of the day a beautifully crafted, 300-page report titled Half Our Future. In essence, the report recognised that there would have to be an increase in public expenditure on the education of what were quaintly called 'the average pupils' – the 50% not adequately catered for in 1963.

There was a clear consensus among politicians, education stakeholders and the wider community that all children should have an equal opportunity to develop their talents and abilities to the full.

John Newsom, very much of his time yet with some foresight, observed:

'Vocational' is a dangerous but indispensable word. It rightly means all that belongs to a man's calling. That itself is no doubt an old fashioned word, but at least it suggests that there is more to a job than money.

Among the report's principal recommendations were that 'the school programme in the final year ought to be deliberately outgoing' and that 'extended technical facilities should be provided whether wholly within the schools or jointly with further education'.

Looking at the contemporary landscape of Further Education, UTCs (Kenneth Baker's brainchild) and schools with technology specialisms, one might surmise that John Newsom would be smiling at the vocational landscape. And yet, and yet.

There must be many readers for whom, on a personal level, leaving school or college and pursuing a vocation meant taking up a calling: to teach, to nurse, to be an architect, to be a minister of the church. There may be others who readily and properly interpret 'vocational' as learning a skill or a trade.

Surely it is time for all of us who are charged with shaping the future for young people to think of vocational education as preparing equally to be an electrician, IT consultant, pilot, banker, restaurateur, car designer, hairdresser or an inspector of prisons. After all, what trades and professions value alike is the ability to get things done to the highest standards.

As in many other contexts in our contemporary world, we find ourselves confined by language and its historical associations. 'Trades' and 'professions' are such an example. We need to bury the vocational-academic apartheid – and its accompanying vocabulary which so bedevils our curriculum and examination frameworks within schools, further and higher education.

England's education provision now stands, by comparison among OECD nations, as a good system. But it remains one where the difference between the highest and lowest achieving groups of students is too great – and wider than that of many comparable nations, including those which practise various kinds of sensible school selection.

We have now had over 70 years of compulsory secondary school education. Yet despite great investment on many fronts, well-conceived national projects (*eg* TVEI), strong regulation of schools and further education, the social-economic attainment gap has narrowed a little in primary schools but widened in secondary schools.

If social mobility, progress and equality are the goals, let us not waste energies on the grammar school debate.

Rather, let us in schools and colleges up and down the country do three things very well: champion applied learning across the curriculum; promote high quality apprenticeships, including as strong alternatives to a university place; and use a vocabulary with students of all ages which promotes parity of esteem between the so-called 'academic' and 'vocational'.

SOFT SKILLS: CAUGHT AND TAUGHT

Confidence, resilience, independence – these companion attributes have become a rallying cry for the many and diverse commentators on social mobility in our schools. The argument runs: get all young people to feel more confident about themselves, to develop their resilience and to hone their independent skills – then so-called 'achievement gaps' will be closed.

Is this the elusive recipe for enhancing social mobility? Is it that easy? And what realistic part can schools play?

The subject of character and soft skills is firmly on the political agenda. While in office Prime Minister David Cameron got Whitehall thinking carefully about measuring happiness in society. The Department for Education produced a well argued report in August 2017 titled 'Developing character skills in schools'; the Education Policy Institute studied employability and soft skills in its excellent research paper 'Educating for our Economic Future', published in October 2017.

And two recent and insightful books on the same subject are well worth dipping into: 'Taught Not Caught' by former Secretary of State for Education Nicky Morgan, and 'The Character Conundrum' by Matt Lloyd-Rose.

What are we talking about here in practice?

Take the following extract from a thoughtfully worded advertisement for new employees to join a five-star international hotel:

The type of person we are looking for can demonstrate:

- *A desire to improve themselves in terms of skills, knowledge and experience*
- *Good organisational skills and high service standards*
- *Patience, a sense of humour and an ability to accept and act on constructive feedback*
- *An ability to work on their own initiative and also to be a good team player*
- *Excellent and pro-active communication skills*
- *An eye for detail and a willingness to improve all aspects of the service we offer*

– A positive attitude to all aspects of the job including enthusiasm, a professional and common sense approach and a dedication to the interests of the business.

If most 18-year-olds were to feel confident enough to apply for such a position, we would probably hail that their parents and their teachers had done a pretty fine job, caught and/or taught.

Take another scenario. Imagine meeting one of your pupils, now aged 11, when they are 25. You meet by chance in a cafe and open a conversation. What do you wish to hear? You may well hope to hear that they continued to enjoy a good education beyond your classroom. More important, you probably want to find out that they are healthy in body and mind, confident, happy and fulfilled – a realisation of many of the soft skills that matter in life.

I have posed this scenario to hundreds of audiences around the world. Irrespective of culture and context, teachers comment on the 'character stuff' and rarely on, say, the young adult's higher education qualifications. In one such audience I recall the headteacher of an internationally famous independent school affirming that by age 25 he expected all his former students to be active and honest citizens, entrepreneurial in their chosen fields, and global in outlook.

We might conclude then that what every parent wants for their child, the nation should want for its children, helped along by experiences at school.

It is rare to enter a school or college which does not – intellectually at least – value 'soft skills', a term incidentally which has its origins in the US army training manuals from the era of the Vietnam War. Whether the school actually teaches the following, implicitly or explicitly, varies markedly: people skills, etiquette, attitudes, social and emotional intelligence, problem-solving, conflict resolution, time management, *etc.*

Some school leaders I encounter contest that these skills and attributes are largely innate, that they are 'caught' from parents, peers, teachers and social media models, and cannot be 'taught'. Others argue that while the nurture element is strong, it is eminently possible to design courses through which soft skills can be taught – indeed, *must* be taught in order that many pupils can enhance their self-esteem and employability.

From years of teaching and observing a range of personal and social education classes, I conclude that, whilst often fun, engaging and containing valuable learning points, even the best planned and executed courses do not contribute significantly to the broader soft skills agenda. They have their place, but not alone.

Rather, the best schools develop pupils' innate character through carefully designed and implemented whole-school values, through their daily ethos, through the dignity of positive relationships between adults and students, through the *consistency* of high expectations. And not forgetting: 'the school's curriculum provides memorable experiences and rich opportunities for high quality learning and wider personal development and well-being' (Ofsted 2009).

A couple of concluding reflections.

First, I came across the following agenda in an outdoor adventure centre. It made me reflect that perhaps soft skills are most effectively addressed away from formal classrooms. The centre judges its own success on the extent to which visiting students leave having absorbed and demonstrated these during their stay.

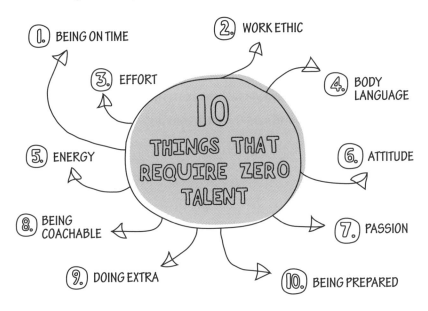

Second, may there always be the space for the originals and mavericks of this world! They might have been inspired by loving or dysfunctional parents, by poor or accomplished teachers, but in the end they shape hard and soft skills to their own inimitable ends. Steve Jobs captured these people best, in relaunching Apple in 1997 (see YouTube):

Think Different

'Here's to the crazy ones.

The misfits.

The rebels. The troublemakers.

The round pegs in the square holes.

The ones who see things differently.

They're not fond of rules.

And they have no respect for the status quo.

You can quote them, disagree with them,

glorify or vilify them.

About the only thing you can't do is ignore them.

Because they change things.

They push the human race forward.

While some may see them as the crazy ones,

we see genius.

Because the people who are crazy enough to think

they can change the world, are the ones who do.'

SPORTING LEGACIES

In common with millions of sports fans around the world my December/ January television viewing has centred on Australia. While the northern hemisphere has been chilled and battered by blizzards, the good folk of Adelaide, Sydney and Melbourne have enjoyed (and endured) sizzling heat and gripping sport.

Courtesy of global TV networks I have been able to watch the greatest test cricket batsman in the world Steve Smith and the top tennis players of the current era, Roger Federer and Caroline Wozniacki. They have not disappointed.

With the arrival of February has come the Winter Olympics in Pyeongchang. Quite apart from the ice-fire pageantry and political symbolism of the opening ceremony where North and South Korea shared a flag, we have been treated to some take-your-breath-away sporting moments. My mind turns to the indomitable skier Lindsey Vonn, to the flying snowboarder Shaun White, to the sublime Canadian ice-dancers Tessa Virtue and Scott Moir. *Citius, Altius, Fortius* in action.

Whenever I watch the world's top sportswomen and men at work, the teacher in me always wonders how they got started, and who inspired them. And I fondly recall one particular individual whom I had the good fortune to come across in my early twenties.

Fred Newton was a quiet, small, modest man. He left a giant sporting legacy in the shape of thousands of boys who played school, district, county, national and international football.

I met Fred when I started teaching at a south London comprehensive in 1973. He was in his seventies then and the pupils affectionately called him 'head of thieving'. He had the uncanny knack of discovering who had taken something from a changing room, and quietly returning the stolen goods to their rightful owner. No fuss. A maths teacher by trade, his entire career in the one school, by the time I knew him he was the school's counsellor and social worker.

He introduced me to Saturday morning football, from Clapham Common and Hackney Marshes to the depths of Ewell and Morden, then Inner London Education Authority playing fields. From the immediate post-war years to the late 1970s, Fred took teams, coached and spotted talent. Generations of boys came under his amateur, expert eye. He believed passionately in sport for all, excellence for some, elite competition for a tiny number.

Over school lunches in the noisy dining-hall of the time, I recall conversations with Fred about sport and physical exercise in general. I loved listening to his reminiscences as I first learned my trade.

We were of a mind that from the first days of a child walking and running, children should be having fun through basic exercise: in the garden, in the park, on the beach.

We shared the view that at primary school enjoyment in keeping healthy, exercise and recreation should be harnessed by teachers through team games, dance, gymnastics and swimming. Cooperation, collaboration and competition should walk hand-in-hand: sport and physical education for all.

The path of course continues for all children into secondary, supported by parents and teachers. For some youngsters, innate talent in some aspect of sport may emerge. The Fred Newtons of this world will spot and nurture that talent. These boys and girls will win races when pitched against their friends, they will excel in dance, skating, judo, rugby or hockey relative to their peers. A handful of them will be talent spotted and find themselves at local clubs, perhaps competing at regional and county finals.

A very tiny minority will join elite squads in their older teenage years and, just maybe, an even smaller number will be selected to represent their country and enter professional sport. The whole process is Darwinian pure and simple: the flourishing of the fittest, the most skilful and the most dedicated.

Children, parents, teachers and club coaches each play their vital part. They always have done and they always will. Opportunity, encouragement, enjoyment and purposeful practice – all are vital. That way lies lifelong involvement and fun in exercise, fitness and sport.

In common with countless teachers down the years, Fred left a special legacy. As I have watched great sporting achievements on TV this past few months, I have thought about teachers who have devoted their time to help children and young people become those who stand tall in international sport.

The joy that sport brings to people throughout life is so often rooted in their experiences in school. In common with thriving arts and music, the presence and promotion of physical education and sport lie at the heart of good schooling – and a life well lived.

A SCHOOL WHICH STANDS OUT

A published Ofsted report I wrote as one of Her Majesty's Inspectors in 2006, as part of the Proportionate Inspection Project (PIP) focused on good and outstanding schools. This was a curriculum-first school.

Overall effectiveness of the school

St Anselm's is an outstanding school which has some special qualities: children whose behaviour and attitudes are exemplary; a staff and leadership team committed to excellence and restless to improve even when they are doing very well; a governing body and interested families equally focused on creating a place of high quality learning and well-being. There is a spirituality which permeates the day-to-day life of the school.

'An excellent primary school that turns out responsible children not just test passers'. 'Teaching and discipline have been consistently good throughout the seven years since reception'. 'Targets are clear and there has been good communication between home and school at all times'. 'An excellent learning environment where my son is able to thrive and reach his potential'.

With very few contrary voices, the quotations above from parents were echoed time and again on questionnaires returned to the inspector. A meeting with parents warmly reaffirmed the extent to which families, many of whom have enjoyed long associations with the school, consider St Anselm's to be a place of high standards, both academically and socially.

What is the cocktail which leads to this success?

First and foremost, children arrive at the school each day wanting to learn. Their self-starters are in very good working order. They take pride in all that they do. They treat one another, their teachers and the environment with dignity and care. They are proud to show their achievements: on the day of the inspection, the reception class presented an engaging assembly, with teachers, families, governors and a priest to guide and

90

support. At the other end of the day, Year 6 pupils were animated and articulate in their discussions about paintings and sculptures they had seen on their visit to the National Gallery, as they prepare for their residential to Constable country. There is both a modesty and confidence about the children which results from their family support and from the way in which teachers bring out the very best in them.

When children arrive in classrooms they encounter learning environments of the highest quality. For example, in every classroom there is at least one display of distinction, whether that of Surreal Dreams in Year 4, London's Burning in Year 2, or Preparation for Our First Holy Communion in Year 3. Lessons throughout the school are underpinned with first-class planning by the teachers; they know the starting points of individual children and track their progress meticulously, with appropriately ambitious targets.

Very good teaching is rooted in warm relationships and high standards of classroom management. Teachers are enthusiastic about their subjects, harness resources (including interactive whiteboards) with skill and enterprise, and pose searching questions which check for understanding. They orchestrate time adroitly so that pupils feel that they are involved with what is going on and what the lesson's outcomes will be. The pupils' listening skills are noteworthy: for example, in a Year 5 mathematics lesson; and in Year 1 and Reception at the end of the day, storytelling sessions were met with rapt attention.

As a result of this consistently good teaching, with a number of outstanding features, all pupils make exceptional progress throughout their years at the school. The 2005 Key Stage 2 test results, for example, record the school being in the top ten per cent of schools nationally in terms of a range of value-added measures. Based on the achievement and attainment tables only, the school in 2005 performed in the top three per cent nationally.

All this success does not just happen. In the words of one parent, the school is led by 'a superb headmaster who is incredibly creative and visionary, and one couldn't wish for a better person to front the show'. The headteacher has led the school with distinction for a number of years and, together with his deputy, knows the school and everyone in it exceptionally well. He has thus been able to make wise judgements about where a new national initiative will benefit the children and when best to stimulate a period of consolidation.

He is surrounded by colleagues who recognise their roles, responsibilities and accountabilities with equal clarity, and who share their expertise openly in a spirit of challenge and support. One feature of the day's inspection was the way in which teachers were willing to debate educational issues and areas of improvement with the inspector, ever with an eye on how their proposed actions would impact on the quality of children's learning.

In particular, the headteacher's 'less is more' file prepared for the inspection reflected both an attention to detail at every turn, and the sense in which valuing people is a cornerstone of how the school is led, managed and run each day. For example, the annual calendar, with its respective roles and actions of headteacher, staff, governors and school association indicates team work of real intent, while a leaflet prepared by governors is purposeful evidence of the rigour with which they hold themselves and senior managers to account.

It is a feature of successful schools that they are restless to improve further. In discussion with staff, there is a self-critical wish to provide a curriculum which engages pupils even more. That said, the school community already enjoys a diverse array of visits out and hosts a range of visitors who enhance the children's awareness of contemporary social, cultural and moral issues. The staff are aware that the small minority of pupils who have English as an additional language need further support, and there is a constant debate about how best to broaden styles of teaching and learning, particularly for some of the most gifted and talented pupils. Tellingly, most parents commented that the school is particularly successful in meeting the needs of all abilities, never making individual children feel they are receiving special treatment.

In a school in which the focus is so resolutely on the pupils, it is perhaps fitting to close this report with their words. In discussions, they are singularly aware of the impact upon them of the Every Child Matters national agenda. They spoke eloquently of how such issues as adoption, healthy eating, serving the community, skills for friendship and buddying have been explored in lessons and with visiting speakers. Indeed, the Year 6 Preparing for Life booklets are a model of their kind.

But what do the children most value about St Anselm's?

'I would like to show visitors how people here work as a group'. 'People here can all join together and get on'. 'In lessons you learn a lot more than you knew before'. 'I'm always learning more about myself'. 'The teachers always help you and make learning fun'. 'I am proud of our writing – all of our writing'. 'We are always working for our charities'.

And if they imagined themselves to be headteacher for the day, what would they change? Very little, although in the opinion of one younger child, 'We should sing more together'.

There is children's joy in learning and teachers' professional pride in a job well done which are evident to any visitor to St Anselm's. The school has moved on most positively since its last inspection, and is very well placed to continue its successes and sustain its mission.

Grade: 1

EDUCATION POLITICS

'What is needed is mutual trust in education: between central government and the teachers, and between local and national politicians. The future success of our schools is one in which governments meddle less, and trust more. And teachers demonstrate an altogether new professionalism.'

'Experience advising education Ministers tells me that practice shapes policy more often than policy shapes practice.'

'Successful politics is about getting four things right: timing, hearts, minds and communication.'

'Short-termism may be the very stuff of Western politics. But it is no longer fit for purpose to address the challenges we face today: good care for the elderly; manageable NHS drug bills; sustainable social housing; viable pensions; funding primary, secondary and tertiary education.'

AN OPEN LETTER TO THE SECRETARY OF STATE

Dear Secretary of State,

In March 1943, Rab Butler, the young president of the Board of Education, went to Chequers to see Winston Churchill, who duly signed off what became the 1944 Education Act.

As you know, the education story since 1944 has been one of conflict and consensus between the government and the teachers of the day. What is needed today and tomorrow is greater mutual trust: between central government and teachers, and between local and national politicians. The successful future of all our schools is one in which governments meddle less, and trust more. And teachers demonstrate an altogether new professionalism.

I have had the privilege of working with many of your predecessors and their Ministers over the past 25 years. Distinguished politicians have their framed photographs on the wall in the foyer of the Department for Education, dating back to Rab Butler, Ellen Wilkinson and the early post-war years. Your photo will one day join them, with your dates inscribed for historians to reflect on.

Your influence over hundreds of thousands of everyday lives will be significant during your term of office, and perhaps beyond. And while I write this letter particularly about schools, I recognise the other significant responsibilities you have for early years, further education, adoption and much besides.

Education featured rarely in the May 2015 election campaign. At local level on the doorstep, voters spoke only of having a good local school – that was their proper message. The British public has rejected politicians who wish to 'weaponise' the National Health Service. When Sir David Nicholson retired from his post as Chief Executive of the NHS in April 2014, he declared that 'the greatest enemy of a flourishing health service is the electoral cycle'.

Many in the education system say the same, that long term planning necessarily eludes politicians with fixed-term contracts. Might you be a pioneer and establish a National Education Service, with a view to taking much of the detail of education practice out of the political arena? What a legacy that would be.

The distinguished brain surgeon Henry Marsh titled his autobiography *Do no harm*, a singular message he wishes to pass on to all surgeons, reminding them of their founding Hippocratic Oath. As the Secretary of State it must be tempting to tinker. Please make sure the first question you ask your DfE and political advisers is: 'Do we need a new policy in education?'

There are two key areas of education policy and practice where we do need your powerful democratic leadership:

1. Establishing a fair funding system for schools across the country. There persists a geographical apartheid in formula funding which your predecessors have long wrestled with. Solutions are not easy, and in an age of austerity relative winners and losers are inevitable. But it cannot be right that a school in Camden receives twice as much as a school in Reading for an 11-year-old, the children living in very similar social contexts. For teachers in the Reading schools, the dice are unevenly loaded, and pupils' outcomes reflect this disparity in budgets.

2. Securing a sustainable stream of good entrants into the profession. Last academic year I travelled the length and breadth of England working with headteachers. Rarely did a day pass without conversations with heads and governors around recruitment, and the disproportionate amount of time and money being spent on securing good teachers for every school. I know from the many outstanding civil servants I meet in your department just how vital a high quality workforce is.

Concentrate please on these two pivotal issues and you will win plaudits from 25,000 headteachers, voters country-wide, and fellow politicians.

Further, if you subscribe to the self-improving school system (rightly championed in the Headteachers' Standards), you might set yourself to be a careful and thoughtful guardian. Don't be tempted to put your indelible stamp on the Office with further initiatives. Rather, leave in five years' time proud to have done no harm, and just a little good.

If you do stray beyond the two areas above, please opt for sustaining and embedding what has been legislated for in recent times: all schools good schools; raised levels of accountability and pupils' achievements; the new curriculum and examination arrangements; pupil premium funding.

And though this counters my plea for little change, dare to be different in just one direction: suspend inspections of good and outstanding schools for one year. Afford headteachers the space to shape that self-improving, self-regulating school system. Then go visit a hundred schools and ask their views.

Since I started my teaching career in a Brixton primary school in 1973, I have learned a few things about change in the workplace. Wise politicians recognise that a cardinal feature of change is that some people will misunderstand or misinterpret what is being presented. Politicians also recognise that when the winds of change blow, some people build walls while others build windmills. And that unintended consequences and events can torpedo the most accomplished planning documents.

Perhaps the celebrated American poet Robert Frost captured it best, when he wrote:

Why abandon a belief
Merely because it ceases to be true?
Cling to it long enough, and not a doubt
It will turn true again, for so it goes.
Most of the change we think we see in life
Is due to truths being in and out of favour.

I'm sure the profession, governors, pupils and parents wish you well in your Office of State. Most of all we wish you continuity in that office, five years in which to see a job well done.

With a little more time, I would have written you a shorter letter. Less is always more.

Yours sincerely
Roy Blatchford

DO NO HARM

I often have to cut into the brain and it is something I hate doing. With a pair of diathermy forceps I coagulate the beautiful and intricate red blood vessels that lie on the brain's shining surface. I cut into it with a small scalpel and make a hole through which I push with a fine sucker. The idea that my sucker is moving through thought itself, through emotion and reason, that memories, dreams and reflections should consist of jelly, is simply too strange to understand. All I can see in front of me is matter. Yet I know if I stray into the wrong area, into what neurosurgeons call eloquent brain, I will be faced by a damaged and disabled patient when I go round to the recovery ward.

Henry Marsh

Memories and dreams as jelly…. – an evocative extract from 'Do No Harm: Stories of Life, Death and Brain Surgery'. Henry Marsh's captivating account of a life spent inside other people's skulls is a must-read for any school leader this summer holiday.

You have to be in the right mood, but the book's key theme captured in the first part of the title resonates as much in education as it does in health. (Marsh's recently published sequel 'Admissions' is equally engaging, especially for anyone contemplating retirement.)

I was an active supporter of the 2010 – 2015 Coalition years: sensible and enabling public policy unfolded, including for schools. This summer a new kind of parliamentary coalition has emerged. Whether it sustains itself or not in its current form, school leaders up and down the country should make the most of the education policy vacuum.

National politicians are unable to do any major policy harm, for fear of losing their jobs. Election manifesto commitments on education from all parties are happily on hold. And I look forward to hearing in the autumn the first major speech of this parliament from Secretary of State Justine Greening. I predict she will start with T-Levels.

So how to fill the void and do some good? My 'less is more' recipe, for summer reflection and autumn action, runs as follows.

1. The NAHT and ASCL should join forces and push hard for the creation of a National Education Service (NES): building a cross-party, cross-nation ambition to establish such a service in England for the coming decades.

As with the NHS, there should be an independent Board and Chief Executive for the NES, charged with taking some of the harmful short-term politicking out of education. Former NHS Chief Executive Sir David Nicholson observed that the worst enemy of long-term planning and serious progress in the NHS is the electoral cycle.

2. Unions and professional associations collectively should impress upon central and local government that the 2017 – 2022 era will be remembered as a time when school and college leaders were left to busy themselves with running their institutions effectively, untroubled by novel policy wheezes from the politicians. We have had several years of productive churn. Let the churn settle and be shaped by schools and academies at 'local' level.

3. Quite simply, teacher recruitment and retention will benefit from a period of calm. The DfE, without other diversions, should pour its considerable energies and skills into securing a supply of great graduates for our primary, special and secondary schools.

4. Experience advising education Ministers tells me that practice shapes policy more often than policy shapes practice. Let the profession embed the curriculum, assessment and examination reforms of recent years, held to account by a wise Ofsted and Ofqual. The profession can make recommendations for gradual change and development, rooted in classroom evidence and students' experiences.

5. Whilst disquiet hangs in the air over the implementation of a national system of fair funding, let altruism and self-interest collide. Thus, some of the uneven per pupil allocations between different parts of the country can be ironed out once and for all.

The time is propitious.

A series of desperate events in the past few months has fractured the country's social fabric in some urban areas. Serious news media coverage has been honest and hard-hitting. Much social media and tabloid journalism has been shrill and vacuous.

In a period of national uncertainty and self-questioning, the *trusted* teaching profession has a unique opportunity. It can move itself, and the many millions of students and families it engages with every day, beyond this volatile climate and lead a spirit of domestic renewal across the country.

A highly influential National Education Service is the vehicle to achieve this prize.

HIGHER EDUCATION UK: A TARNISHED JEWEL

It might be argued that British Prime Ministers and American Presidents in office share one particular trait in common: their popularity overseas outshines their favourable ratings at home. Think Thatcher and Blair, Clinton and Obama from the modern era.

Higher Education in the UK currently finds itself in a similar place: highly respected overseas, but an increasingly tarnished jewel at home.

Working internationally, I encounter leading educationists in several nations. Many senior politicians, top civil servants in education departments, principals of schools and colleges across the globe have spent what they describe as memorable and enjoyable years in British universities.

Their experiences range from initial degrees to MAs, MScs and PhDs. They will frequently comment on the warmth of welcome they received from fellow students, the high quality of their tutors, the proper intellectual demands of the courses, the robustness of the degree awarding process.

These are sound reasons why large numbers of universities around the world seek to establish faculty and research partnerships with UK universities. In turn, this has been matched by the significant expansion of British Universities overseas, with campuses springing up across the globe to cater for students hungry for the product and reputation they offer.

Suffice to say, the holding of a British University degree – and what it implicitly says about the holder's good command of English – provides a strong professional passport back in the home country. And of course the holder has paid handsomely into UK coffers as an overseas student for that qualification.

Thus, a system highly respected and cherished abroad. But what is the picture at home?

I recall working with Lord Dearing on his landmark 1997 report 'Higher Education in the learning society'. Such was the esteem in which he personally was held that the introduction of the annual £1,000 fee went through almost on the political nod. And raising it to £3,000 a few years later seemed a matter of pragmatism if targets to open up Higher Education to a much wider group of 18-year-olds were to be achieved.

University vice-chancellors attest that the introduction of fees moved the whole HE system onto a more sustainable footing, able to compete globally. Proper investment in teaching and learning, research, faculty, and facilities followed. Competition for top world rankings from the USA, Europe and Asia meanwhile has intensified.

Twenty short years on from Dearing, what has gone wrong, to the point where at home opprobrium from all quarters is being poured upon the university sector?

First, the major hike in undergraduate fees to £9,000+ per annum has rightly drawn a sharp focus on value for money. Whilst those studying sciences enjoy acceptable contact hours with tutors and in laboratories, many arts and humanities students have documented that they meet a tutor all too infrequently and sit in overcrowded lectures.

Second, the value-for-money focus has also shone a light on some highly variable teaching. By any measure, teaching quality in schools has been transformed over the past decade. Students moving from accomplished A level teaching into university seminars of mixed quality have not been slow to make comparisons.

Third, the pastoral care systems of a number of top universities have been shown to be wanting, with respect to both home and international students. In particular, clumsy press handling of a few high profile suicides has drawn stinging criticism from student unions.

Fourth, the new Teaching Excellence Framework, whilst flawed, has been treated in a cavalier spirit by certain universities resting on historic reputations. Their irritated response to being awarded a *bronze* rather than the presumed *gold* has served only to reinforce students' views that complacency characterises too many universities.

Fifth, the unacceptable gap between many academic staff's salaries and those of the senior management has not surprisingly raised uncomfortable questions, including about poor governance.

Sixth, and potentially *the* issue poised to cause genuine havoc across the UK Higher Education sector, are the intolerable behaviours of the government-owned Student Loans Company and the legislation which has allowed inexorable rises in interest rates on loans.

An unfortunate cocktail has emerged: students (and their parents) to whom I have spoken recently perceive that they are receiving a higher education experience that is mixed in quality, overpriced and led by complacent, overpaid vice-chancellors. And social media are stirring the pot.

In the pause of August and as the new academic year beckons, there is an urgent need for university and political leaders to turn their gaze towards resolving all of the above. Their time is short. Vice-chancellors' jobs are on the line.

The much treasured jewel of British Higher Education is currently tarnished. It would be good to think that, over the coming years, home students can feel as good about our HE system as the rest of the world still does.

A FAILURE OF POLITICS NOT POLICY DIRECTION

Successful politics is about getting four things right: timing, hearts, minds and communication. And in announcing during his March budget speech that all schools *would* become academies, the Chancellor of the Exchequer got all four wrong.

Timing: well surely this was not his announcement to make. To pluck out of the policy firmament a statement that, whether governors liked it or not, their school would become an academy by the end of the parliament was certainly bad political timing. The ground had simply not been prepared. And had he forgotten he was anyway in the middle of a European debate destined to split his party?

Hearts: by early 2016, the hearts of governors and headteachers had been warming to the momentum of the voluntary academy movement, taken at the right pace. But the Chancellor's sudden assertion that academies were the *only* solution significantly under-estimated the fair response from many leading councillors in successful local authorities – which in turn fuelled professional and parental opposition to the idea.

Minds: headteachers think and care deeply about the schools and the communities they lead. Many heads of good and outstanding schools have not to date been persuaded of the educational merits of academy conversion, and the budget speech did nothing to engage with the intellectual arguments for academisation.

Communication: in politics, it almost doesn't matter what someone is saying; what really matters is what the listener is hearing. And what headteachers, parents, councillors and professional associations heard up and down the land was a Chancellor seeking to pepper a budget speech with a headline for the following day's papers. What they heard was not a considered view about an important educational matter.

So an educational initiative that arose in the Blair years to crack chronic school failure in inner urban settings became, at a mistimed stroke,

Conservative Party policy for the lifetime of this parliament, not having been in the party manifesto.

By contrast with her hapless Chancellor, Nicky Morgan has listened wisely. Her decision to reverse the compulsory move is well judged.

She has had to withstand some pretty sustained attacks in recent weeks as a result of the poisoned chalice of a clumsy policy she was handed. She initially tried to back the Chancellor's edict, but it rapidly became clear that parliamentary arithmetic was going to defeat her. Thus came the politically adroit and skilfully worded announcement from the Secretary of State on Friday:

I am today reaffirming our determination to see all schools to become academies. However, having listened to the feedback from Parliamentary colleagues and the education sector we will now change the path to reaching that goal.

By focusing our efforts on those schools most at risk of failing young people, and encouraging 'good' and 'outstanding' schools to seize the opportunities of conversion, we will ensure the continued growth of the academy programme, empowering frontline heads and school leads, and transforming even more children's education.

Taken together with significant assurances to backbenchers that small rural schools will not close unless both local and national government agree, the short political storm has been deftly managed. Back to Brexit, as it were.

The sadness about all this failure of politics is that, since local management of schools (LMS) in the 1980s, elected politicians of left and right have been on an inexorable path to create 24,000 independent-state schools. That has been the policy direction. Readers with good memories may recall it happened at a stroke in the early 1990s with the Further Education Colleges moving out of local authority control.

Whether Rab Butler and Alec Clegg are turning in their graves today is another matter. Clearly, the notion of a 'national system, locally administered' is being recast. The fact is, as I wrote in 2014 in *The Restless School*, the UK school system is in for a decade of churn as all schools are destined to move to independent-state status.

By 2022 a mature relationship between all academies and local and central government will be secured. We shall have a well established, self-improving school system rooted in the practised capacity of groups of schools to challenge, review and support one another's standards and professional needs.

The word 'academy' will no longer haunt us, nor be an unhelpful dividing line between schools and local and national politicians. And just whisper it: a Secretary of State for Education will be able to enter an Easter conference and not run the risk of disrespectful heckling, which has been the recorded experience of Shirley Williams, David Blunkett and almost every Secretary of State since the 1980s.

'All political life ends in failure' runs the old maxim. Let us hope that Nicky Morgan's recent announcements on academies ensure she can lead the education system through this parliament without too many more alarums caused by her Cabinet colleagues.

WHY LONDON'S EDUCATIONAL WEALTH SHOULD BE SHARED

The House of Commons Education Committee received a report in January on the role of Regional Schools Commissioners. Nothing exciting there and it may have sunk with little trace given the government's more pressing business. But among the report's recommendations is one to be resisted fiercely.

The report concluded first, that 'the division of London between three RSCs is unnecessarily disruptive'; and second, 'the government should redesign the RSC regions so that they are coterminous with Ofsted regions, including creating an RSC for London.' This is wrong on both counts.

London's education history

In common with capital cities around the world, the history of London's education and schooling has been bravely pioneering, highly politicised and, at turns, a story of abject failure and significant success for its children and young people.

The London School Board which existed between 1870 and 1904 was responsible for that great civic investment in school buildings. Anyone who has been taught in, or been a teacher in one of the great three-decker primary schools which stand proudly on so many street corners across London will testify to their merits. The Victorians built to last. They created airy (some would say draughty) classrooms and large halls which to this day provide vibrant, spacious, colourful learning environments. And of course they placed the windows skilfully above desk height, so pupils had to focus on the teacher.

The London County Council (LCC) took over responsibility between 1904 and 1965, and skilfully managed a system through two world wars, including the extraordinary evacuee programme of September 1939 when 1.5 million children were sent to rural locations considered to be safe.

The post-war baby boom arrived. With the coming of comprehensive education in the 1950s, the LCC pioneered the opening of Kidbrooke

School in 1954, and other schools followed years ahead of the wider comprehensive movement in the 1960s. The critique from the right was immediately that replacing the grammar schools with huge, impersonal education factories was a mistake led by a socialist desire for a classless quality education. Lines in the educational landscape were drawn which remain today.

Soon after the Inner London Education Authority (ILEA) was created in 1965, it enjoyed the leadership of men like Sir Ashley Bramall and Sir Peter Newsam who stirred in young teachers like me a passion for great comprehensive education, and backed us with superb resources and facilities. There was an all-too-brief heyday.

By the mid-1970s, things had soured badly. The combination of teacher shortages, militant union action, members' ideological interferences, and a sprawling bureaucracy covering the inner London area led to some of the larger comprehensives simply being ungovernable. I taught in one. Despite the considerable educational innovation and the best endeavours of many hard working staff, national politicians took a close look and eventually shut down the ILEA in 1990.

The inner London boroughs then became education authorities in their own right, and remain so today. One might make the cautious judgement and say they began to restore parental confidence in local schools, though primaries never suffered reputational damage in the way the large comprehensives had.

Sharing successes

London Challenge was born in 2003 under the Labour Government and unashamedly declared that it would create a step-change in the performance of London secondary schools. And thus it proved: a well-executed, sustained whirlwind of school improvement, subsequently built upon by a number of high profile academy sponsors with considerable financial largesse.

Which returns me to London's educational wealth and why it should be shared.

By any measure, London's schools in 2016 are in good heart: parental confidence is high, student satisfaction rates are equally positive, teachers enjoy working in the schools and are well remunerated, and bespoke programmes for leaders are world-class. Look no further, for example, than the excellent 'The 9 Pillars of Greatness' produced by the London Leadership Strategy. Education in the capital remains politicised (a lazy media is never far away) but is enjoying a golden era.

That is *not* to say that on my recent travels to Sheffield, Bristol, Colchester and Liverpool I have not encountered exciting teaching and learning, and outstanding leaders who are shaping the self-improving school system, frequently against the odds. Of course there is great practice throughout the nation. Those who work within the confines of the London Underground zones should go learn from it.

I have teased Cambridge secondary heads that you cannot speak to them at a conference for more than eight minutes without one of them raising the question of school budgets, and rightly so. While a new 'fair funding' formula is set to be rolled out nationally, the apartheid of funding between schools operating in inner London and in the rest of the country continues.

Islington, Camden and Hammersmith and Fulham, to take three examples, enjoy an annual funding of about £6200 per pupil. For Warrington, Dorset and West Sussex the figure is about £4200 (Source: ASCL, 2014-15 budgets, excludes pupil premium funding). Just imagine for a moment, if you teach in Warrington, what an additional £2000 per pupil – wisely spent – could add to a child's education in your school.

It's never just about money. But part of London's current and much celebrated educational achievement *is* resource-led. Those resources are enabling leaders and teachers in the capital's primary and secondary schools to create systems, cultures, classroom materials, experiences for pupils that are more difficult – not impossible – to realise in contexts of constrained budgets.

I am a member of the Headteacher Board for the aptly titled *East England and North-East London Region*. And there are two other Boards which serve to link London with the shires. Over the past 18 months since our creation we have seen a number of examples of highly successful educational bridges built between inner London schools and those which lie in the surrounding boroughs and counties.

The outreach needs to go further. The clear message of this work to date, with its positive impact on thousands of pupils, is that any attempt by government to create an inward-facing London RSC would be a profound mistake. This is *no* time for London to look inwards.

In the same way that London Challenge created great networks for school transformation, so now and into the future London must share its 'educational wealth' and face outwards. London's schools need to be altruistic. Leaders and teachers in the capital city should commit to supporting their fellow practitioners in coastal areas, towns and isolated rural communities which lie within their geographical reach and influence.

Who knows? We might also find that those coastal town schools can teach London teachers a thing or two.

SCHOOLS MUST CONSIDER DOUBLE SHIFTING

The latest Department for Education data confirms what headteachers and local authority leaders have been saying for the past few years: we need to rethink how we provide school places.

Growth in immigration, combined with the baby boom, is putting unprecedented pressure on the school system across the country. There was a 1.3% increase in student numbers in state and independent schools in England between January 2014 and 2015. This growth has been most keenly felt in state primary schools, where there has been a 2.1% increase in numbers – equivalent to almost 94,000 more children – in the past year.

This has led to super-sized schools, as highlighted in the BBC profile on Gascoigne Primary in Barking, the largest primary school in England where the pupil roll totals 1,200. Today, there are 87 primary schools with more than 800 students, compared with 77 in 2014 and 58 in 2013.

The government has committed to opening 500 new free schools over the next five years to ease pressure. This will go some way to housing the rising number of four-year-olds as we nudge to a UK population of 77 million by 2050, but it won't go far enough. We also need fundamentally to rethink the school day and teachers' working patterns.

The orthodoxy of all primary pupils starting at 9am and finishing at 3.30pm has to be challenged. In the same way that early years' settings offer morning and afternoon places, many urban primaries will need to think along similar lines for all their students. This form of double-shifting is common in other countries, and will become the norm in England's major cities.

Take the Indian High School in Dubai, with its enrolment of 12,000 students and fleet of 81 air-conditioned buses to transport pupils and staff. Different grades and ages operate different shifts across a 7.30am to 6.50pm timeframe. In recent years, I have seen similar arrangements in Egypt, India and the USA, sometimes for religious reasons (with girls and boys attending the same school but at different times of the day), sometimes because of a shortage of school buildings, sometimes as a result of bold and creative educational thinking.

In the UK, a number of state and independent schools have consciously changed working hours for older students to reflect when they are at their most alert. At Hampton Court House in Surrey, for example, sixth form lessons start at 1.30pm and finish at 7pm. The later start time helps their teenage brains and the condensed day affords students more independence over how they structure their time, opening up a huge range of work experience and community service opportunities, off-peak gym times and sport coaching.

Local authorities and academy providers should start planning now for how the school population can be differently provided for, using time in school more efficiently. Terms could be lengthened as required: four to eight-year-olds could attend school from 7.30am to 12.30pm, and nine to 11-year-olds from 1.30pm to 6.30pm.

In secondaries, lessons for 11 to 14-year-olds could run from 7.30am through 12.30pm, and from 1.30pm to 6.30pm for older students. Or, as in Californian high schools, students sign up for different 'tracks', depending on which nine months of the year they choose to be in school.

The teachers' unions will huff and puff; teachers' contracts will need reshaping, but thousands more teachers are needed anyway over the next decade and this will provide increased employment opportunities. Students, parents, governors and the wider community will need to be educated about the new realities of shift schools; childcare provision in particular will need to be reconsidered as working families wouldn't be able to rely on schools looking after their children during working hours.

Crucially, from my observations internationally, school buildings and resources will need skilful husbandry. Within the next few years many primary and secondary schools in urban areas will be opening their doors 24/7, for formal schooling and a wide variety of adult and community learning. The precious resource which is the local school will not stand idle for many weeks of the year as it currently does.

In times of financial constraint and a significantly increasing student population, for politicians and school providers alike, what are the alternatives?

TEACHERS VS GOVERNMENT: 70 YEARS OF EDUCATION POLICY

('Teachers vs Government: 70 Years of Education Policy', presented by Roy Blatchford, was broadcast at 8pm on Radio 4, 22 April, 2014)

In March 1943 Rab Butler, the Young President of the Board of Education went to Chequers to see Winston Churchill. After a weekend of playing bagatelle, dining and watching films of Tsarist Russia, Butler found a moment alone with him.

Churchill leaning back on his pillows in a four poster bed, night-cap on and with a large cat at his feet was an unlikely beginning for the most fundamental reform of the English education system, but that night the prime minister signed off on what became the 1944 Education Act.

Conceived during the Blitz and the Normandy Landings, it is remarkable to think that in the darkest days of 1944, civil servants and Ministers were focused on post-war reconstruction to build, as they saw it, the new Jerusalem. Churchill, in one of his inimitable radio broadcasts to the nation, described the Act as "the greatest scheme of improved education that has ever been attempted by a responsible government".

Seventy years on, the legacy of the Education Act is still widely felt. For Michael Barber, who as head of Tony Blair's delivery unit introduced strategies and targets to the nation's classrooms, Butler's Education Act was not only seminal in 1944, it still resonates today. 'It's very hard to do today what Butler did in the 1940s, build a consensus and then make the change, simply because of the nature of the modern world. If you try to build a consensus now, the world moves before you've had time to do the reform'.

Today we accept free primary and secondary education as a national birth-right. But pre-war things were very different. There was no duty placed upon parents to send their children to school, and most pupils left school at 14. Butler's Act introduced compulsory education to 15, with a clause to raise it to 16; any fee-paying was forbidden; and the church schools were brought within the national system.

So the 1944 Education Act provided real chances of social mobility, something educationists ever since have tried to build on. While many argue today's education system hinders social mobility, one of the most positive legacies of the Act was the opportunities it gave people they otherwise would not have had.

Colin Cutler, aged 87, says passing the 11-plus and attending Maidenhead grammar school via a scholarship, changed his life and thousands of young people like him. 'The fees at that stage were five pounds a term. And there was no question that that was a good bit higher than my father's weekly wage at that time. So it wouldn't have been on the cards if I hadn't got a scholarship'.

But passing the 11-plus didn't necessarily guarantee working class pupils would take up their place at grammar school. Baroness Shirley Williams, who was Secretary of State for Education between 1976 and 1979, says: 'I had several friends whose parents couldn't afford uniform. They never went to grammar school at all. Others didn't go because they were expected to stay until at least 15 and their parents wanted them to come out as quickly as possible to get jobs'.

The past is a foreign country – we did things differently then.

A documentary broadcast on Radio 4 charts the unfolding of the education system to the present day, and finds a system where all too often the government of the day was pitted against the teaching profession.

The 1950s and 1960s are remembered today by teachers and headteachers who taught through those decades as a period of common purpose and rebuilding after the war. After all, many had served in the forces and were determined to create an enduring peace.

The Butler Act had established a national system for education from Northumberland to Cornwall, but with the power for implementing change delegated to local education authorities and revered chief officers, such as Alec Clegg in the West Riding. Clegg toured Yorkshire inspiring teachers and making it very clear who was running education in his area. This was an era of considerable teacher autonomy and little accountability to parents.

Today Ministers argue that, after the New Labour years of targets and centrally driven strategies, teachers once again enjoy freedoms to teach as they choose, in return for greater accountability. The scrapping of local education authority powers has been a badge of office for Secretaries of State from Kenneth Baker to Gove.

What disturbed the post-war consensus was a mild but radical request from the Labour government in 1965 to abolish selection at 11+. Shirley Williams is in no doubt to this day that the creation of comprehensive schools across the country through the late sixties was the most important step forward for education in the 20th century. 'The survival of the comprehensive idea has been extraordinary. The Tories in the end haven't dared to go back to selection. I'm waiting to see whether they will'.

Kenneth Baker, Secretary of State 1986 – 1989, thinks otherwise: 'The Labour party went for comprehensivisation which proved to be a great mistake because Harold Wilson's 'grammar schools for all' is simply not attainable. It was thought up travelling on the tube from Hampstead and it was a mistake'.

The teaching profession largely welcomed the move to comprehensives, and rather aimed their strikes of the early and mid-1970s at improving pay and conditions – and successfully too.

In 1976 Prime Minister James Callaghan launched the Great Debate at Ruskin College, Oxford. 'The traditional concern of the whole Labour movement is for the education of our children and young people on whom the future of the country must depend'. It is clear that the speech was against a backcloth of union militancy which made him genuinely nervous of entering the teachers' so-called 'secret garden'.

Callaghan stepped where no previous government politician had ventured. He suggested there should be a National Curriculum. It took the Baker Act 12 years later to introduce that, Blunkett to revise it, and the current Coalition to recast it again, although not making it a compulsory requirement for academies.

Williams in the 1970s, like subsequent education secretaries, felt the displeasure of the teaching profession at close quarters. 'Going to education conferences was to be crucified,' recalls Williams. 'You got spat at, you got shouted at, you got abuse hurled at you'.

Butler's legacy remained relatively unscathed until the 1988 Education Reform Act. In many ways, it dismantled what Butler had created, with directives from Whitehall about curriculum and testing, the birth of GCSEs, and the advent of local management of schools which challenged the historic role of local authorities. Now headteachers and governors had control of their budgets, and teachers naturally became nervous of pay and conditions being worked out by individual schools rather than through national agreements.

But if Baker was controlling, Blair and Blunkett were even more centrist and interventionist when they delivered the 'Education Education Education' mantra in 1997. Where the Butler Act was localist, New Labour actively challenged schools' autonomy through targets, strategies and league tables which overwhelmed the profession. Relations with the teaching unions hit a nadir, with ballots and strikes in the late 1990s. Blunkett is unapologetic: 'If you're going to bring about change, you're going to break eggs, and the grump in the staffroom was always going to have one foot in the grave'.

Today, Michael Gove seems just as happy to incur the wrath of teachers. Sir David Bell, Permanent Secretary at the DfE under both Labour and coalition governments, tells the programme: 'There was clearly a quite significant attempt by the coalition government to reset the relationship with the trade unions'.

Bell goes on to say that Michael Gove was very clear with civil servants at the Department for Education on his appointment that getting the academies act through very quickly was important because 'he wanted to make that early statement that he fundamentally believed in the autonomy of schools and therefore more schools should be given academy status'.

Despite all the criticisms of recent education reforms under both Labour since 1997 and this coalition government, notwithstanding academies, free schools and excessive testing of pupils, schools are unquestionably better places to be for pupils and teachers alike than they were immediately post-war. There is now an investment in state education which Butler and Churchill could only have dreamed about. And while largely scrapping the grammar/secondary modern system in favour of comprehensives may not have cracked social mobility challenges, university participation has risen in a way the reformers in 1944 could not have imagined.

Governments of all colours since 1944 have shown they cannot resist pulling power to Whitehall. What Baker, Blunkett and Gove have devolved with one hand, arguably they have taken back to the centre with the other.

There are signs of course that some sort of local leadership is reasserting itself with the appointment this month of a high-powered team of Regional Commissioners to oversee academies, in a move reminiscent of Butler's vision for LEAs.

What will the education system look like in 70 years' time?

David Blunkett – who has been reviewing education policy for Labour – is clear about his party's next steps in our programme. When I asked him whether he thought the future would lie in 25,000 independent state schools, he replied: 'I think the changes are irreversible although we'll want to build on them and we'll want to reintroduce the glue. So academies are here to stay....but we need something like the Cleggs of West Yorkshire rather than the Cleggs of the modern era'. He is rejecting the idea of thousands of schools working alone, rather a rejuvenation in counties or regions of ambitious and inspiring political and headteacher leaders.

National politicians since 1944 have been unable to resist tinkering and sometimes meddling in the nation's classrooms. Greater autonomy has often felt like it has come with conditions attached – you are free to run your own schools as long as you do it the way we want you to.

At times, teachers have responded naively and crudely – Michael Gove is certainly not the first Education Secretary to bring them out of the classroom on to the street in protest.

The story since 1944 has been one of conflict and consensus, with varying degrees of intensity. What is needed is mutual trust in education: between central government and the teachers, and between local and national politicians. The future success of our schools is one in which governments meddle less, and trust more. And teachers demonstrate an altogether new professionalism.

WHO SITS AT THE INTERNATIONAL TOP TABLE?

'CleverLands' by Lucy Crehan is a seriously important book on 21st century global education.

The text is destined to be much quoted and widely debated. It is handsomely written, and combines engaging personal travelogue with trenchant research. With her first person narrative and disarming title, the author has pulled off something original in educational studies.

Her starting point was professional frustration working in an inner London comprehensive, where systems of accountability strangled her own and fellow teachers' best efforts and practices. So she set out to interrogate first-hand what she describes as 'the world's education superpowers' as measured by their performance in PISA – international tests in reading, maths and science for 15-year-olds. (The author is quick to point out that school success is not only to be measured in international test results.)

Would the grass be greener, for students and teachers, in Canada, Finland, Singapore, China or Japan? Spending what a friend described as 'a geeky gap year', Crehan engagingly invites herself into schools across three continents. And she sees keenly, informed by her evident research knowledge of psychology and how motivation plays in learning.

On a personal note she concludes that Canada, with its sense of balance between the teaching of academic content and broader social and moral skills and traits, and balanced accountability for school leaders, is where she would choose to educate her own future children. On a professional educator front, she concludes that each of these countries has much to teach the rest of the world about how they organise and deliver primary and secondary schooling.

To quote a few examples amongst many. Visiting Finland the author is singularly impressed by the focus on play in the early years, and by the high quality of support for children with special needs. In Japan she is struck by their deep belief that everyone is intellectually equal, and by the thoughtful use of 'lesson study' in schools.

In Singapore, it is the exemplary teacher training and role of Master Teachers which draw the author's eye, while in China students' work ethic and the maths lessons of demonstration, modelling and practice impress her. And in Canada it is kindergarten quality, positive relationships in schools, and approaches to assessment and accountability which are distinctive.

The harsh discipline of Japan's junior high schools, undue pressure on young Singaporeans, exam cheating in China, the over-emphasis on discovery learning in Canada – these aspects are covered with an equally questioning eye, the author seeking to disentangle stereotype and reality through social conversations with parents and students.

Chapter 17 is titled 'Five Principles for High-Performing, Equitable Education Systems' (note the adjective 'equitable') and one which national and international researchers will readily seize upon. Crehan identifies with conviction what she concludes are the key ingredients of built-to-succeed school systems: getting children ready for formal learning; designing curricula contexts for mastery; supporting children to take on challenges, rather than making concessions; treating teachers as professionals; combining school accountability with school support.

The book's analysis of each of these ingredients is open-minded, perceptive and well judged. Naturally the reader in England will reflect how much of this cocktail applies to our own education system. For a wider audience, can politicians and education leaders, in any jurisdiction, cherry pick the best features from elsewhere and embed them in a different society?

Reading and rereading Crehan's excellently referenced text, I am left pondering two key inter-connecting questions.

First: *Is relative decline inevitable in high performing school systems?*

Most readers of 'Cleverlands' will be familiar with the work of Jim Collins. In his best sellers 'Built to Last' and 'Good to Great' Collins celebrated the achievements of major US companies in the 1980s and 1990s. However, into the 21st century, many fell from grace, reputation and profitability, about which he was subsequently moved to write in 'How the Mighty Fall'. Collins identified 'five stages of decline' from hubris born of success, through denial of risk and peril, to irrelevance or death.

Crehan chose her five countries to visit based on the 2012 PISA results. The recently published 2015 results indicate that these countries remain more or less at the top table, though Finland has dropped out of the Top 10 in maths (and what is going on in Estonia?!). Will the trends continue through the 2020s and 2030s?

Readers familiar with Albert Hirschman's writings will recognise this line of questioning. Hirschman argues that organisations are conceived to be permanently and randomly subject to decline and decay, to a gradual loss of efficiency and energy, no matter how well the institutional framework within which they function is designed.

Second: *Can certain countries ever join the top table?*

Crehan concludes her vivid panorama of five significant education systems with the words: 'To attribute these countries' enviable outcomes to culture and dismiss their value as models would be a grave mistake. Culture can change'. She optimistically cites examples from Finland, China and Singapore where schooling and teaching were once less highly prized than they are today.

Can the author realistically envisage countries such as Mexico, Tunisia and Indonesia (low attainers in 2015 PISA rankings) ever making that *cultural leap* to transform systems in order that their students compete with those in Japan, Korea and New Zealand? World leaders are asking that very question.

In my experience of international education, culture does indeed trump systems. No matter what education reformers may do, even inspired by this book, for some time to come PISA's upper echelons will stay out of reach to young people born in certain global settings.

THE PROSPERITY INDEX

Over the past five years I have spent ten 'tours of duty' establishing school inspection frameworks in different parts of the world. What countries introducing such frameworks have in common is the ambition to create world-class learners among their young people. Nothing less than establishing outstanding schools to deliver those ambitions will do.

Leaders in these countries are developing a deep understanding of the cocktail of a modern successful nation, with aspirational education targets at the core. One source they are borrowing from is the Legatum Prosperity Index. It looks at eight aspects of a thriving society:

- Economy
- Social Capital
- Entrepreneurship & Opportunity
- Health
- Education
- Personal Freedom
- Safety & Security
- Governance

The Index compares such diverse components as average life satisfaction, corruption perceptions, secure internet servers, GDP and hospital beds. Currently, Norway occupies 1st place, Switzerland is 8th, the UK is 13th and Russia is 59th. Make of those what you will.

Visiting Abu Dhabi in the United Arab Emirates this month, it is fascinating to read the Education Council's ambitions for 2030: 'To produce world-class learners who embody a strong sense of culture and heritage and are prepared to meet global challenges'.

And, even more far-reaching, is their vision for a highly educated and cultured society 2070 – 'beyond oil'.

Such countries are of course able to fix a clarity of mission without some of the messiness of Western democracies. They are constructing 21st century nationhood without the complex historical baggage of an Industrial Revolution, Empire, and two World Wars which have irrevocably shaped our own destiny.

What is clear however is that their leaders are seeking to bring into thoughtful balance the eight aspects of the Prosperity Index. Education policy is not seen as separate from that which shapes social capital, entrepreneurship and governance. There is joined-up planning at the highest levels, rooted in a long-term vision.

Returning to a tourist-submerged Whitehall this week, and walking past various ministries before turning into the Department for Education, I couldn't help a flight of fancy. Imagine an away-day for the Permanent Secretaries of these ministries to examine the UK's prosperity index. What is each of them advising their respective Secretaries of State to do which *complements* another's Department of State?

The Prime Minister has made us look keenly at general well-being and happiness alongside GDP – and has sadly been lampooned for his efforts. He is right to make us look in a more rounded way at the crowded islands we inhabit. His Whitehall colleagues should also be more outward-facing, glimpse what is happening in the East, and refashion policy and practice.

Short-termism may be the very stuff of Western politics. But it is no longer fit for purpose to address the challenges we face today: good care for the elderly; manageable NHS drug bills; sustainable social housing; viable pensions; funding primary, secondary and tertiary education.

Here's to 'prosperity' wearing a different hat, rooted in longer-term political visions.

THE RESTLESS GLOBE

Trick(y) Question: Which is the fifth largest 'country by population' in the world today, and will be the third largest by 2050?

Answer: After China, India, USA, and Indonesia, the fifth largest 'country by population' today is 'all the peoples of the world who are living in a country that is not the one they were born in'.

Scientists generally agree that about 70,000 years ago, Sapiens from East Africa spread into the Arabian peninsula, and from there quickly overran the entire Eurasian landmass. The history of humankind is one of restless migration. We happen to be witnessing at present, often in grim media images, that natural human characteristic – but that restless urge to move has always been with us. We have long been global citizens, divided by our nation states.

Pundits and commentators in all spheres of human endeavour like to compare peoples and nations, and build news stories around international comparisons. Take the recently published Portland index of so-called 'soft power': the ability to achieve influence by building networks, communicating compelling narratives, establishing international rules and drawing on the resources that make a country naturally attractive to the world. Well, the UK comes 1st out of 30; Finland is 15th; China 30th.

In education, the international comparators come fast and furious. We can quote PISA (reading, maths and science) or TIMSS (maths and science) to cheer us up one year or depress us the next. Last year's report from the Organisation for Economic Co-operation and Development (OECD) on literacy and numeracy proficiency placed Korea and Spain at the top, the US and UK at the bottom of a list of 21 countries. Yet another report suggested Britain could add trillions to its economy if it only had the education standards of Poland, Vietnam and Estonia.

We routinely position polar opposite ideas in order to determine which is right. Whenever we follow this process the result is people on both sides trying to thrust their views forward. Positions harden rather than consensus being achieved.

Let us take the debate promoted by a TV documentary set in a Hampshire secondary school where students experienced the Chinese way of doing. Have no doubt, Asia including China is indeed the 'Asian Tiger'. It pulsates with optimism and evidence of rapid progress is visible at every turn. Education merely reflects this wider ambition. Each generation is a fresh start and all students have the chance to exceed the achievements of their parents. Their overall expectations are high and they deliver.

The Confucius education tradition has a proud history and dictates that education should encourage the student to think about how he should live his life and interact with others, and the forms of society and government in which he should participate. It's not just learning facts but it does place the onus on the student to make the most of what they are offered. This is where the idea that the Chinese value hard work comes from. They do, but so do Singapore and Hong Kong. They believe that hard work rather than background – or even innate ability – is the key to success and that anyone who wants it can achieve it.

So why are they seeking advice from Hampshire educationalists? Well the answer is that we have our own proud tradition.

At its best our education system develops individuals who can think for themselves. They are encouraged to question and debate ideas and the result, when done well, is that we produce students who can innovate and problem solve as well as having strong subject knowledge and expertise. Note our very successful creative industries and our record for innovation in all fields as opposed to just routine production.

Yet, both we and Shanghai have our problems. In Asia the challenge is to find an educational style that builds on their success but at the same time encourages the problem solving and innovative thinking which prepares people for leadership in a complex world. In the UK our education tradition seems to create a mixture of excellence and mediocrity as it is much more teacher and school dependent. It's harder to manage students who think for themselves and question the teacher.

Maybe what we should be taking from Asia (and Poland and Estonia) is their belief in the power of hard work and their belief in students' ability to succeed. And helping students to understand that *they* need to take some ownership for their own progress, enjoy the fact that difficulty in any kind of learning is pleasurable, and pursue the route to mastery.

We are restless people wanting to improve how we do things, in all walks of life. We can learn much from other countries and adopt some of their ideas. But wholesale transfer never works – education is context related and reflects a country's society and ambitions. And in the UK, we should remember to champion our 'soft power'.

(With acknowledgements to Deborah Eyre)

SUCCESS IS A JOURNEY

I recently addressed an audience comprising the leaders of the Arabian Gulf's petrochemical industries. The buzzword at the conference was 'diversification'. The price of a barrel of oil hovers around $60, where once it was over $100. The leaders of the Gulf nations need the wealthy oil companies to help their economies diversify. They look with envy at the way research-led science parks, bustling with innovators, have spun off from major UK universities thereby creating considerable wealth for the nation.

My theme was about government, education and industry working to common goals. In particular, I stressed the point that as well as diversifying their economies they need to invest in education. And they all are doing just that – with education at the heart of their 2030 and 2040 visions of sustainable societies 'beyond oil'. *Sustainability* is the mantra.

It is instructive to see which particular aspects of a successful education system they are choosing to embrace. Success is a journey, and each country is at a different stage of planning and delivery. I would identify seven priorities they are variously following through on.

1. Investing in teachers

There is unanimous recognition that in the most successful global systems, teachers are well trained, respected by parents and trusted by politicians. But to be a teacher, particularly for men, is not a natural career path in some cultures. The equivalent of Teach First is being tried, but cultural shifts are not easy. What *is* being acknowledged is that the remuneration of teachers in government schools needs a considerable lift if, as part of diversification, the brightest and best are to take up the teacher's vocation.

2. Investing in leaders

The same rings true for leadership. Education ministries are realising that a systematic approach to high quality leadership training is a *sine qua non*. Principals and senior teachers are being given appropriate mentoring and tailored courses, with a special emphasis on teaching and learning, and moving them away from their traditional role as administrators. Links between international and local government schools are paving the way. School leaders I've met are responding enthusiastically.

3. Kindergarten: a running start

The reputation of fine early years work in much of northern Europe has persuaded many governments in the Gulf Region that investment in kindergarten is vital. Publicly and privately funded systems are emerging, many rooted in the UK's best early years practice, many borrowing the best from Montessori. How cultures through history have educated very young children has varied, but today most countries hold to this vital, formative period for a child being a shared enterprise between the family and the state.

4. 21st century Curriculum

Local, national and international dimensions underpin the best curriculum in any jurisdiction. For countries with textbooks and workbooks which form the core of classroom teaching, change is gradual. Content is being updated to ensure a careful balance between 'old' and 'new'. And countries across the globe rightly want to modernise without westernising. Two aspects of curriculum development though are on the march across the Gulf: digital empowerment leading to blended learning for students; and the classroom of tomorrow being bilingual in Arabic and English.

5. International Benchmarking

The impact of TIMSS, PISA and PIRLS in recent years offering respected international comparators is not to be underestimated. In countries without the traditions of long established, independent national examinations, looking outwards for external validation of students' outcomes becomes increasingly important. Where countries feature in international league tables matters to them, and provides a stimulus for further government investment in schools. In a climate of business diversifying, what others across the globe are doing assumes a particular resonance.

6. Vocational and technical training

A feature of a number of countries driving for world-class education – notably some of those formerly in the USSR – has been their well judged investment in vocational and technical education, closely linked to local labour markets. Establishing appropriate qualification frameworks has been an integral of the process. The oil-rich nations have observed this and are following suit. Persuading business to set aside budgets for traineeships and apprenticeships is imperative, and an arena where government, industry and education must collaborate.

7. Graduation and post-graduation rates, research and innovation

There are no Gulf universities in the world's top 200. But the ambition is there. Business leaders, who themselves have often enjoyed an education in some of the best universities in the US and UK, know with a passion that their own higher education sectors need to step up to the mark. As the oil business helps economies in the region diversify, so it must do all it can to press the case for a research and innovation dividend located in public and private universities. The collaboration imperative is again self-evident.

Looking at this list of seven priorities from a UK perspective, one can feel professionally proud without being complacent. The best I see in schools and universities across the UK suggests that what others in the world are pursuing in educational planning and delivery, we have been pretty smart at for a good few decades now.

Perhaps it takes a period working outside the UK to appreciate just how successful our own education system, with all its wrinkles, really is.

PART TWO

TEACHERS' STANDARDS

Guidance for school leaders, school staff and governing bodies

Preamble

Teachers make the education of their pupils their first concern, and are accountable for achieving the highest possible standards in work and conduct. Teachers act with honesty and integrity; have strong subject knowledge, keep their knowledge and skills as teachers up-to-date and are self-critical; forge positive professional relationships; and work with parents in the best interests of their pupils.

Part One: Teaching

A teacher must:

1. Set high expectations which inspire, motivate and challenge pupils

- establish a safe and stimulating environment for pupils, rooted in mutual respect
- set goals that stretch and challenge pupils of all backgrounds, abilities and dispositions
- demonstrate consistently the positive attitudes, values and behaviour which are expected of pupils.

2. Promote good progress and outcomes by pupils

- be accountable for pupils' attainment, progress and outcomes
- be aware of pupils' capabilities and their prior knowledge, and plan teaching to build on these
- guide pupils to reflect on the progress they have made and their emerging needs
- demonstrate knowledge and understanding of how pupils learn and how this impacts on teaching
- encourage pupils to take a responsible and conscientious attitude to their own work and study.

3. Demonstrate good subject and curriculum knowledge

- have a secure knowledge of the relevant subject(s) and curriculum areas, foster and maintain pupils' interest in the subject, and address misunderstandings

- demonstrate a critical understanding of developments in the subject and curriculum areas, and promote the value of scholarship

- demonstrate an understanding of and take responsibility for promoting high standards of literacy, articulacy and the correct use of standard English, whatever the teacher's specialist subject

- if teaching early reading, demonstrate a clear understanding of systematic synthetic phonics

- if teaching early mathematics, demonstrate a clear understanding of appropriate teaching strategies.

4. Plan and teach well structured lessons

- impart knowledge and develop understanding through effective use of lesson time

- promote a love of learning and children's intellectual curiosity

- set homework and plan other out-of-class activities to consolidate and extend the knowledge and understanding pupils have acquired

- reflect systematically on the effectiveness of lessons and approaches to teaching

- contribute to the design and provision of an engaging curriculum within the relevant subject area(s).

5. Adapt teaching to respond to the strengths and needs of all pupils

- know when and how to differentiate appropriately, using approaches which enable pupils to be taught effectively

- have a secure understanding of how a range of factors can inhibit pupils' ability to learn, and how best to overcome these

- demonstrate an awareness of the physical, social and intellectual development of children, and know how to adapt teaching to support pupils' education at different stages of development

- have a clear understanding of the needs of all pupils, including those with special educational needs; those of high ability; those with English as an additional language; those with disabilities; and be able to use and evaluate distinctive teaching approaches to engage and support them.

6. Make accurate and productive use of assessment

- know and understand how to assess the relevant subject and curriculum areas, including statutory assessment requirements
- make use of formative and summative assessment to secure pupils' progress
- use relevant data to monitor progress, set targets, and plan subsequent lessons
- give pupils regular feedback, both orally and through accurate marking, and encourage pupils to respond to the feedback.

7. Manage behaviour effectively to ensure a good and safe learning environment

- have clear rules and routines for behaviour in classrooms, and take responsibility for promoting good and courteous behaviour both in classrooms and around the school, in accordance with the school's behaviour policy
- have high expectations of behaviour, and establish a framework for discipline with a range of strategies, using praise, sanctions and rewards consistently and fairly
- manage classes effectively, using approaches which are appropriate to pupils' needs in order to involve and motivate them
- maintain good relationships with pupils, exercise appropriate authority, and act decisively when necessary.

8. Fulfil wider professional responsibilities

- make a positive contribution to the wider life and ethos of the school
- develop effective professional relationships with colleagues, knowing how and when to draw on advice and specialist support
- deploy support staff effectively
- take responsibility for improving teaching through appropriate professional development, responding to advice and feedback from colleagues

- communicate effectively with parents with regard to pupils' achievements and well-being.

Part Two: Personal and professional conduct

A teacher is expected to demonstrate consistently high standards of personal and professional conduct. The following statements define the behaviour and attitudes which set the required standard for conduct throughout a teacher's career.

- Teachers uphold public trust in the profession and maintain high standards of ethics and behaviour, within and outside school, by:
    - treating pupils with dignity, building relationships rooted in mutual respect, and at all times observing proper boundaries appropriate to a teacher's professional position
    - having regard for the need to safeguard pupils' well-being, in accordance with statutory provisions
    - showing tolerance of and respect for the rights of others
    - not undermining fundamental British values, including democracy, the rule of law, individual liberty and mutual respect, and tolerance of those with different faiths and beliefs
    - ensuring that personal beliefs are not expressed in ways which exploit pupils' vulnerability or might lead them to break the law.
- Teachers must have proper and professional regard for the ethos, policies and practices of the school in which they teach, and maintain high standards in their own attendance and punctuality.
- Teachers must have an understanding of, and always act within, the statutory frameworks which set out their professional duties and responsibilities.

© Crown Copyright 2011

MASTER TEACHER

This Standard should be read as part of a profile of a Master Teacher who may have his or her own particular strengths in specific areas. Above all, a Master Teacher is someone whose professionalism has come to be seen as an integral part of his or her character.

Master Teachers are excellent teachers, deeply committed to making a difference to the lives of their pupils. The Master Teacher is a self-assured presence in the classroom, who effortlessly captures pupils' imagination.

Although Master Teachers may take on management and other roles in the school, there is no presumption that they will move outside the classroom. They are exceptional practitioners, for whom high levels of performance in the basic Teachers' Standards are taken as given. They are enthusiastic about their specialism or subject(s).[1] They have a strong sense of the significance of what they teach in the context of the whole curriculum and beyond.

A. Knowledge

Master Teachers have deep and extensive knowledge of their specialism, going far beyond the set programmes they teach. They have an intrinsic curiosity about their specialism, keep up with developments, and their teaching reflects their own passion and expertise. They respond intelligently and confidently to the unexpected and wide-ranging questions their pupils are encouraged to ask, and they are able to lead discussions and explorations which take pupils beyond the confines of teaching programmes.

They are able to teach their specialism clearly, intelligently and inventively, showing considerable breadth and initiative. They have a keen sense of the most effective and engaging ways of communicating the subject matter to pupils of all abilities and aptitudes.

Master Teachers are reflective and self-critical regarding their own

1 In the rest of this document, references to "specialism" should be taken to mean "subject(s) or specialisms".

teaching and make critical appraisals of new developments and techniques, which they use judiciously. A thorough understanding of the developmental and social backgrounds of pupils further supports and informs their practice.

B. Classroom Performance[2]

Master Teachers command the classroom, skilfully leading, encouraging and extending pupils. They have the respect of both pupils and parents. They are at ease in their role, and discipline and dialogue are unselfconscious and effective.

Teaching is motivating, often inspiring, and basic principles are expertly taught. Expectations are challengingly high, realistic, based on sound experience, and take into account the abilities of all pupils. The pacing of lessons is well orchestrated and transitions between whole class teaching, group and individual work are seamless. Questioning and discussion are of a high order, relevant and at times deep.

Pupils are consistently focused and engaged in their studies, and are encouraged effectively to reflect on their own progress. Homework and independent study activities are wisely chosen to extend the range and depth of pupils' knowledge, understanding and acquisition of skills. Master Teachers ensure that high quality assessment and feedback are consistently prompt, rigorous and constructive. They enable pupils to identify and remedy their misunderstandings and build on their successes. They promote pupils' desire to seek and apply their knowledge further.

C. Outcomes

The Master Teacher's meticulous planning and organisation ensure that pupils are well-prepared for all forms of assessment. Outcomes achieved by pupils in the context in question are outstanding. They have an awareness of school, national and international benchmarks and examination reports, including data from maintained and independent schools.

Master Teachers have an extensive understanding of and expertise in relevant assessment systems and examinations. They make critical use of

2 *"Classroom" should be read as extending to all other environments in which Master Teachers work.*

data, relating to the prior and current performance of pupils, to underpin and motivate improvement. As a result, pupils understand what they are learning and have a strong grasp of the principles on which the knowledge and capacities in question are based.

Outcomes are also outstanding in a more informal sense. Pupils not only understand what they have been taught and its significance, and are able to deploy this knowledge critically and analytically, but they are inspired to go beyond what they have been taught.

D. Environment and Ethos

The class is one in which pupils feel welcome and valued. There is a stimulating culture of scholarship alongside a sense of mutual respect and good manners. The Master Teacher has an excellent rapport with classes and with individual pupils.

The classroom environment created to support study and activities is an inspirational example of practice, appropriate to the age range or phase. Resources, including books and IT, are well-chosen and stimulating, contributing significantly to progress in lessons. Resources excite, extend and support different abilities, interests and aptitudes.

In classrooms for younger pupils, visual stimuli arising from children's own work offer powerful models to which other children can aspire. In classrooms for older pupils, scholarship is also evident in the classroom surroundings. Displays often reflect contemporary events and a breadth of subject matter which extend beyond the subject under study.

E. Professional Context

Master Teachers are highly regarded by colleagues, who want to learn from them. They willingly play a role in the development of school policies and in the professional life of the school. They work in collaboration with colleagues on pastoral and wider pupil-related matters, giving advice as appropriate. They engage with and contribute to professional networks beyond the school.

They are analytical in evaluating and developing their own craft and knowledge, making full use of continuing professional development and appropriate research. They recognise the vital importance of out-of-school and extra-curricular activities, both academically and personally, and play a leading role here and in the wider life of the school.

Master Teachers are open in the giving and receiving of professional advice, which may include coaching or mentoring colleagues and less-experienced teachers. They work to significant effect with other adults in ensuring high quality education for the pupils they serve.

© Crown Copyright 2011

NATIONAL STANDARDS OF EXCELLENCE FOR HEADTEACHERS

Purpose

The *National Standards of Excellence for Headteachers* (2015) define high standards which are applicable to all headteacher roles within a self-improving school system. These standards are designed to inspire public confidence in headteachers, raise aspirations, secure high academic standards in the nation's schools, and empower the teaching profession.

The context for headteachers changes constantly. In most contexts, a headteacher has led one school; in some settings headteachers are responsible for leading more than one school. Job titles are various – including principal, executive, associate and co-headteacher – as are the governance arrangements to which headteachers are accountable.

These standards are intended as *guidance* to underpin best practice, whatever the particular job description of the headteacher. They are to be interpreted in the context of each individual headteacher and school, and designed to be relevant to all headteachers, irrespective of length of service in post.

The standards can be used to:

- shape headteachers' own practice and professional development, within and beyond the school
- inform the appraisal of headteachers
- support the recruitment and appointment of headteachers
- provide a framework for training middle and senior leaders, aspiring to headship.

The Teachers' Standards (2011, as amended), including the Personal and Professional Code of Conduct which applies to all teachers, provide a foundation upon which the standards for headteachers are built.

Preamble: the role of the headteacher

Headteachers occupy an influential position in society and shape the teaching profession. They are lead professionals and significant role models within the communities they serve. The values and ambitions of headteachers determine the achievements of schools. They are accountable for the education of current and future generations of children. Their leadership has a decisive impact on the quality of teaching and pupils' achievements in the nation's classrooms. Headteachers lead by example the professional conduct and practice of teachers in a way that minimises unnecessary teacher workload and leaves room for high quality continuous professional development for staff. They secure a climate for the exemplary behaviour of pupils. They set standards and expectations for high academic standards within and beyond their own schools, recognising differences and respecting cultural diversity within contemporary Britain. Headteachers, together with those responsible for governance, are guardians of the nation's schools.

The Four Domains

The *National Standards of Excellence for Headteachers* are set out in four domains, beginning with a Preamble. There are four 'Excellence As Standard' domains:

- Qualities and knowledge
- Pupils and staff
- Systems and process
- The self-improving school system

Within each domain there are six key characteristics expected of the nation's headteachers.

Domain One

Excellent headteachers: qualities and knowledge

Headteachers:

1. Hold and articulate clear values and moral purpose, focused on providing a world-class education for the pupils they serve.
2. Demonstrate optimistic personal behaviour, positive relationships and attitudes towards their pupils and staff, and towards parents, governors and members of the local community.
3. Lead by example – with integrity, creativity, resilience, and clarity

– drawing on their own scholarship, expertise and skills, and that of those around them.

4. Sustain wide, current knowledge and understanding of education and school systems locally, nationally and globally, and pursue continuous professional development.

5. Work with political and financial astuteness, within a clear set of principles centred on the school's vision, ably translating local and national policy into the school's context.

6. Communicate compellingly the school's vision and drive the strategic leadership, empowering all pupils and staff to excel.

Domain Two

Excellent headteachers: pupils and staff
Headteachers:

1. Demand ambitious standards for all pupils, overcoming disadvantage and advancing equality, instilling a strong sense of accountability in staff for the impact of their work on pupils' outcomes.

2. Secure excellent teaching through an analytical understanding of how pupils learn and of the core features of successful classroom practice and curriculum design, leading to rich curriculum opportunities and pupils' well-being.

3. Establish an educational culture of 'open classrooms' as a basis for sharing best practice within and between schools, drawing on and conducting relevant research and robust data analysis.

4. Create an ethos within which all staff are motivated and supported to develop their own skills and subject knowledge, and to support each other.

5. Identify emerging talents, coaching current and aspiring leaders in a climate where excellence is the standard, leading to clear succession planning.

6. Hold all staff to account for their professional conduct and practice.

Domain Three

Excellent headteachers: systems and process

Headteachers:

1. Ensure that the school's systems, organisation and processes are well considered, efficient and fit for purpose, upholding the principles of transparency, integrity and probity.

2. Provide a safe, calm and well-ordered environment for all pupils and staff, focused on safeguarding pupils and developing their exemplary behaviour in school and in the wider society.

3. Establish rigorous, fair and transparent systems and measures for managing the performance of all staff, addressing any under-performance, supporting staff to improve and valuing excellent practice.

4. Welcome strong governance and actively support the governing board to understand its role and deliver its functions effectively – in particular its functions to set school strategy and hold the headteacher to account for pupil, staff and financial performance.

5. Exercise strategic, curriculum-led financial planning to ensure the equitable deployment of budgets and resources, in the best interests of pupils' achievements and the school's sustainability.

6. Distribute leadership throughout the organisation, forging teams of colleagues who have distinct roles and responsibilities and hold each other to account for their decision making.

Domain Four

Excellent headteachers: the self-improving school system

Headteachers:

1. Create outward-facing schools which work with other schools and organisations – in a climate of mutual challenge – to champion best practice and secure excellent achievements for all pupils.

2. Develop effective relationships with fellow professionals and colleagues in other public services to improve academic and social outcomes for all pupils.

3. Challenge educational orthodoxies in the best interests of achieving excellence, harnessing the findings of well evidenced research to frame self-regulating and self-improving schools.

4. Shape the current and future quality of the teaching profession through high quality training and sustained professional development for all staff.

5. Model entrepreneurial and innovative approaches to school improvement, leadership and governance, confident of the vital contribution of internal and external accountability.

6. Inspire and influence others – within and beyond schools – to believe in the fundamental importance of education in young people's lives and to promote the value of education.

© Crown copyright 2015

PART THREE

BLINKS

www.blinks.education

High quality reviews for the education sector

A   What are Blinks?

- *Blinks* offer high quality reviews of educational settings: nurseries, schools, colleges, university departments. The process aims to get to the heart of a setting, capturing students' lived experience.

- *Blinks* involve one or two-day visits focused on improving the quality of offer to students. Frequently there is an emphasis on consolidating good and excellent practice.

- *Blinks* are rooted in best national and international practice, and are tailored to each individual context. 'Less is more' and 'working alongside' are guiding principles.

- *Blinks* are led by experienced leaders and practitioners in their fields, all of whom have operated in the UK and internationally and have worked together on the Blink methodology.

- *Blinks* provide leaders with: professional development in self-evaluation, a written report evaluating educational quality, and a supportive agenda for future directions.

B   Background

Blinks (short inspections) were first developed by Her Majesty's Inspectors in England's schools.

The *Blinks* team has extended the range over the past 15 years to include nurseries and kindergartens, schools and academy trusts serving all ages, further education colleges and university courses.

In overseas contexts, *Blinks* have been commissioned in government, private and international schools and university departments.

Common areas of focus for *Blinks* include:

~ students' progress in lessons and seminars

~ teaching and learning experience

~ curriculum and ethos

~ oracy and literacy

~ middle and senior leadership

~ institution self-evaluation and inspection preparation

~ high performance learning.

C   What do leaders say about Blinks?

'We commissioned one-day Blinks for 30 of our primary schools to help headteachers with sharp self-evaluation. Student outcomes and inspection results improved significantly for almost all participating schools.' (Local Authority Director)

'Blinks were conducted over a three month period across 15 of our primary, special and secondary academies, with a focus on the consistency of our ethos and enriching the curriculum for students. The process and the final reports were invaluable for leaders and teachers.' (Academy Trust Regional Director)

'Our family of seven schools serving students from around the world moved into the very good and outstanding inspection categories as a result of the week of Blinks. Fun and professionally engaging.' (CEO, International Schools)

'The Foundation Year provision at the university has been radically overhauled since we commissioned the Blink. Students and faculty found the 'working with' style of those leading the Blink enabling and positive.' (Head of College)

Further information about *Blinks* is available at www.blinks.education

D   Examples of Blink Reports

(names have been changed)

Example 1: Longworth Primary School

Dear Kavita and Staff

I last visited the school in May 2015 and you have all clearly taken significant strides since then on the school improvement journey. By common consent, the Ofsted report of June 2015 caught you at your best; and the inspection itself was expertly led by your senior team.

In essence, what you have done over the past 12 months is secure that good judgement and ensure consistency of provision across the school which has benefited all children. This consistency is rooted in wise and reflective leadership, judging the optimum pace at which pupils, teaching and support staff have been able to move forward. There is an altogether sharper environment for learning than a year ago and, for example, transitions in lessons waste no time. There is some very good teaching rooted in detailed planning, superb resources and animated questioning to which pupils respond in kind. Many pupils are well able to articulate what they are learning and why, and to explain to a visitor the full range of work they have been covering in recent months, as evidenced in the attractive wall displays.

You have established clear systems and expectations as a framework for the day-to-day commerce of the school. (Gone is some of the careless practice I saw previously, to be replaced by *careful* practice, and less clutter!) Colleagues unanimously welcome that clarity and the way that it is modelled by the headteacher. Leadership responsibilities and accountabilities at all levels in the school are understood, and acted upon thoughtfully; investment in well focused CPD has been successful.

Judicious attention has been paid to thorough and regular assessment procedures, and preliminary consideration has been given to 'life beyond levels'. Studying and discussing your curriculum planning for the 2016-17 academic year suggests that this aspect will emerge as a distinctive strength of Longworth, affording rich and memorable learning for all pupils. Indeed, the emphasis on a learning environment which aspires to include all comers is another hallmark of the school; that aspiration is not yet fully realised.

The dedicated work by staff continues, with that aspiration for 'excellence as standard'. Your partner secondary school – from my recent visit there – has secured many, many excellent features, and I don't doubt that focused partnership work across the 4 – 16 campus is key to raising standards further at Longworth; recent art work is but a forerunner.

As you open doors for primary children so that they enjoy an inspirational learning journey, you might wish to reflect on the following points.

- *If it ain't broke, don't fix it.* There are many aspects of the academy's provision (noted above) which are securely good, so you'll want to sustain and embed those.

- In securing good provision in every classroom, you will want to ensure that a small minority of pupils engage fully in tasks when they are expected to work independently. *(What does great independent learning look like?)*

- There is a need to focus on a programme of 'coaching to outstanding', so that good teachers become excellent – this is just one area where partnership 4 – 16 will pay dividends, as scholarship, expert subject knowledge (*eg* in mathematics) and intellectual enquiry become increasingly embedded in Key Stage 2.

- There is some exceptional extended writing in Reception – now to render the exceptional more commonplace, and you have the passionate early years' leadership to deliver that. There is a parallel need to radically reshape and invest in the relatively poor outdoor learning area.

- As you shift the culture of the academy to value equally the needs of the more and most able pupils alongside those with special educational needs, you will no doubt look keenly at how you promote articulacy, 'mastery', high quality outcomes/products, learning journals (we discussed Kirby Muxloe *www.kmprimary.leics.sch.uk* School21 *www.school21.org* and Red Oaks *www.redoaks.org* as possible models).

- And the jewel in the crown? Your outdoor learning area genuinely has the potential to be 'stand out'; wise investment in the physical lay-out and how creative curriculum planning can link to it will surely reap considerable benefits for rich, mixed-age learning.

Finally, you are very well placed to shift gear as leaders: to sustain, excite and disrupt in equal measure. I know you will pursue tenaciously those ambitions towards excellence and a learning community wherein 'everyone is challenged to achieve their personal best, in an environment where every lesson, every day is good or better, supported by 360° of care, support, love and challenge.'

I look forward to revisiting the school and hearing about the future successes enjoyed by both pupils and staff.

Good wishes

Roy Blatchford

Example 2: Crendon Academy

Dear Alex and Colleagues

'The past is a foreign country. They do things differently there.'

There are a good number of staff and students at Crendon Academy who can recall different days, when the school was much less of a place than it is today. As of April 2017, the school is very popular with local families and a place which professionals want to join. This is a school at ease with itself where to be a student, teacher, parent or visitor is to be part of an educational community steering knowingly towards excellence. There is an attention to detail and ambition for constant improvement which permeate.

Teachers and leaders have a shared and confident understanding of the school's values and expectations; in all parts of the organisation, staff reflect creatively on their practice and appreciate the distinctive contribution of each and every colleague. The school's investment in high quality professional development is palpable.

With the same sense of focus and purpose, students go about their daily studies, treating one another and staff with courtesy and mutual dignity. The learning environments – from the entrance foyer, to cabinet displays in corridors, to some exemplary classrooms – speak well of the collective endeavour, with an emphasis on each achieving his or her personal best, in a climate of care, support and love.

During a day of visits to classrooms, I encountered real joy in learning; highly skilled revision sessions, fit for purpose at this time of the year; youngsters deep in their personal reading; students being challenged to address complex historical and geographical questions; senior students immersed in their chemical experiments; others reviewing meaningfully the results of internal examinations and their requisite, personal next steps. Purposeful practice is a hallmark.

Schools are a people business, and the excellent leadership which is to be found in all quarters at Crendon knows well that positive development and step-change are about orchestrating a judicious blend of timing, encouragement and appropriate challenge. *So is now the time to reflect again on L.P. Hartley's words which head this letter?*

The past is the pre-occupation with the C/D borderline. The future is the 18% of grade 9s!

By common consent, the junior students have a potential about them which needs grasping, with urgency. An altogether raised level of expectations for academic achievement – rooted in teachers' own scholarship and promotion in classrooms of intellectual enquiry – is called for, across all subject areas.

Hand-in-hand must go a concerted effort by all staff to promote greater articulacy and social confidence in the students, many of whom will otherwise continue to rest content within narrow horizons. This, to my mind, is not about social engineering, but about affording greater social capital to all the youngsters served by the academy.

As Principal and staff you must surely be very proud of what you are achieving day by day, term by term. Teaching and running schools is a relentless and highly enjoyable business. The families you serve must surely be talking in their neighbourhoods about the good local school. And if, according to one educational commentator, 'an excellent school delivers superior performance and has a high impact over a sustained period of time', then that goal is within your certain grasp over the coming period.

Thank you for sharing the school with me.

Yours sincerely,

Roy Blatchford

Example 3: University Language Centre

A   Context

As a key part of the wider transformation plan, changes have been made to the English Language curriculum experienced by foundation year students. There are approximately 1450 students, currently divided into Level 1: 700 students; and Level 2: 750 students.

Students receive 13 hours of classroom-based teaching. Class sizes (setted by language ability) are generally 30–35 students; National Geographic book, video and audio resources are the core 'texts'.

Three observers visited five sessions, talked to staff and students, and examined students' workbooks.

B   Key points from observations

- The majority of students arrive at lessons ready to learn and sustain their focus throughout the 50/100 minute time slots. Sessions generally start on time.

- Teaching is competent, rooted in strong subject knowledge, and using the target language of English consistently; Arabic is used judiciously to support weaker students and ensure good pace to the lessons. Teachers prepare well for the sessions.

- The National Geographic materials – books, videos, tapes – are highly engaging and relevant for the age range, motivating staff and students alike. Reading, writing, speaking and listening skills are valued equally. Investment in this new course has been timely and well judged.

- Classroom environments are satisfactory, with some positive displays of 'students at work' on the corridors.

- There is clear evidence of teachers' effective marking of students' work, and of students using the formative marking to improve their own written English.

- Students indicate that they are using the on-line facilities for between 5–7 hours a week, to embed and extend their learning of English.

- The overall atmosphere and culture in the Centre are harmonious and purposeful, and have undoubtedly seen a step-change under new leadership since a year ago.

C   Next steps

In taking forward the Centre's practice, consideration might be given to the following:

- How can teachers best interest 'the boys in the back row', many of whom are at risk of failing the course through lack of engagement?

- How might teachers, particularly at this stage of the term, 'speak less' and expect students to '*speak more*, in full sentences'?

- What techniques of 'question and answer' might be used to ensure that male and female students engage orally with one another across the classroom?

- How might teachers inject more humour and energy into sessions by asking students to teach and model language points, particularly where students are growing in confidence and competence in their spoken English? *Have fun with relishing new vocabulary, and get everyone to join in!*

- What 'standard technique' (eg a summary notice-board to be photographed by students) might be introduced into every teaching session so that all students can take away the key learning points of the session? This point links to....

- How might iPads, Podcasts, mobile phones, *etc* be harnessed for appropriate learning, say in a five minute 'digression' every session?

- 'Do you see what I see?' How can the faculty introduce through CPD mutual classroom observations which strengthen everyone's daily practice?

D   Leadership discussions

Discussions with the Centre's leadership team included the following:

- There are well judged plans to develop a programme of CPD for faculty.
- The Centre might benefit from a modest increase in administrative staff.
- National Geographic might be able to support the improvement of displays in classrooms, particularly focused on key language points and helping students understand a map of the world.
- The forthcoming 'Book Club', with movies, and the general raising of the profile of the new Resource Centre, possibly staffed by a couple of advisers/counsellors.
- Further work needed on supporting students 'at risk', particularly related to their attendance.
- A Steering Committee to be established to ensure effective co-ordination across English, Maths and IT teaching and learning in the foundation year.

My thanks to co-observers for their open discussions and leadership of this review, and my especial appreciation to teachers and students for sharing their classrooms.

Roy Blatchford

ACKNOWLEDGEMENTS

To a handful of leading thinkers, do-ers and commentators on education who continue to influence my thinking and writing: Geoff Barton, Rebecca Clark, Jo Coton, Tim Coulson, Kate Dethridge, Deborah Eyre, Richard Howard, Peter Hyman, Juliette Jackson, David Laws.

To my father, aged 94, who started teaching in 1948. He was a headteacher from 1957 to 1985 in Bath, Marlborough, Worcester and Southampton. His proof-reading, research and editing skills remain invaluable. He would want me to add: if there are errors in this collection, they are mine.

To a number of colleagues in different countries who have taught me about their cultures and education systems.

To the thousands of teachers and students whose classrooms, home and abroad, I have enjoyed during *Blinks*.

To Alex Sharratt, a nimble and creative publisher whom I have found to be, over many years now, a strong advocate for schools, their teachers and leaders.

To Mark Evans for his drawings on pages 23 and 85.

ABOUT THE AUTHOR

Roy Blatchford is founder of www.blinks.education – working with schools, colleges and universities in the UK and internationally. He has spent the past two years implementing education system reform in the Middle East.

Roy was Founding Director (2006–2016) of the National Education Trust, an independent foundation which leads excellent practice and innovation in education.

Previously he served as one of Her Majesty's Inspectors of Schools (HMI) in England, with national responsibilities for school improvement and for the inspection of outstanding schools. He has extensive experience of writing inspection frameworks, nationally and internationally, and has reviewed over 1000 schools and colleges in Europe, USA, Middle East and India.

For 30 years Roy has been an international trainer and conference speaker on English and literacy, school improvement, leadership and curriculum development. He has been an adviser to various UK governments, including Deputy Chair of the DfE Teachers' Standards Review (2011) and of the Headteachers' Standards Review (2014). He is a member of the Education Policy Institute's advisory board.

Roy began his teaching career in London, moving to be Principal of schools in Oxfordshire and Milton Keynes. He is a Fellow at Oxford Brookes University, has been a Visiting University Professor in the USA, and is co-founder of the Mumbai-based education foundation Adhyayan. He is the author/editor of over 150 books.

Roy was appointed CBE for services to education in the 2016 New Year Honours.